GIANTS

THE UNFORGETTABLE SEASON

GIANTS

THE UNFORGETTABLE SEASON

Text by Kevin Lamb

Macmillan Publishing Company
New York
Collier Macmillan Publishers
London

Prepared and produced by the
Creative Services Division of NFL Properties, Inc.,
10880 Wilshire Blvd., Suite 2302, Los Angeles, CA 90024
for the Macmillan Publishing Company,
866 Third Avenue, New York, NY 10022.

The names, helmet designs, and uniforms
of the NFL Member Clubs are registered in the
U.S. Patent and Trademark Office.

Printed and bound by Dai Nippon, Tokyo, Japan.

First printing, June 1987

1   2   3   4   5   6   7   8   9   10

Library of Congress Catalog Card Number: 87-61221

ISBN: 0-02-589020-4

Vice President & Creative Director: David Boss
Director-Publishing Operations: Scott Kabak
General Manager: Bill Barron
Editor-in-Chief: John Wiebusch
Managing Editor: Chuck Garrity, Sr.
Art Director and Designer: Glen Iwasaki
Associate Editor: Jim Perry
Art Assistant: Joanne Parsh-Fuller
Director-Manufacturing: Dick Falk
Manager-Print Services: Tina Thompson
Manager-Production Services: Jere Wright

CONTENTS

1925–1986

FROM HUMBLE BEGINNING TO SUPER END

KING OF THE HILL, 'TOP OF THE HEAP'

By the end of the season, the Giants were big enough in New York to rest their elbows on the twin towers. They owned the city lock, stock, and Gatorade barrel. So what if they played their games across the Hudson? That mattered only to mayors and tax collectors. The Giants were New York's team, part of New York's soul, and it was to New York that they brought back the NFL championship that had been loaned out for 30 years.

It all started at Minnesota in November. On fourth-and-17, the Giants had one last chance. It had about the same odds of connecting as a message in a bottle. But what do you know? New York made the first down. Bobby Johnson caught Phil Simms's pass for a 22-yard gain, and Raul Allegre's field goal won a game that had been lost. There was light at the end of the Lincoln Tunnel after all.

But maybe it didn't start then. Maybe it started before that.

Maybe it started the previous January, at Chicago's Soldier Field, where the Giants fell from the playoffs and vowed not to let it happen next year. "If there was one game that let us know where we were going to be, that was the game," Harry Carson said.

Maybe it started three years earlier, amid the debris of the 3-12-1 collapse of 1983. That was when coach Bill Parcells decided to collect players who never would be overpowered again. He hired strength and conditioning coach Johnny Parker, who assembled a practically bionic team in the new $200,000 weight room. After the Giants' 39-20 comeback victory over Denver in Super Bowl XXI, tight end Mark Bavaro said, "We just came out in the second half and wore them down."

Maybe it started in 1978, when the franchise scraped bottom after The Fumble. From the smoke swirling around an airplane banner and the ashes of disgusted fans' tickets, general manager George Young emerged to plot a course to the top. He hired Ray Perkins, then Parcells. He drafted Simms, Lawrence Taylor, and Joe Morris for all the right reasons. That was when the Giants started behaving again like a real football team.

Or maybe it started with the teams of the late 1950s. If not for them, there would have been no tradition for the teams of the 1970s to smear. There would have been no fond memories for long-suffering Giants fans to fall back on. Even the coach was one of them. Parcells was 17 on December 28, 1958, when he watched The Greatest Game Ever Played. He cried after Alan Ameche plunged one yard on third down for the Baltimore Colts' 23-17 victory over the Giants, 8:15 into overtime. "I know it sounds corny," he said 28 years later, "but I'm a very lucky guy to live two miles from where I grew up and to be coaching this team in the championship game."

Pro football began in New York. The NFL was organized in Canton, Ohio,

of course, but it never really began until 73,000 people filled the Polo Grounds December 6, 1925, to watch Red Grange play for the Chicago Bears against the new pro football team in New York. In 1927, the Giants won their first NFL title with an 11-1-1 record. In 1934, the Giants came from behind to beat Chicago 30-13 on an icy field for their second NFL championship. Do you really think that 27-point fourth quarter would have made folklore as the Sneakers Game if it had happened on the home field of the Portsmouth Spartans? The Giants won again in 1938, beating Green Bay 23-17.

The Giants won the 1956 championship, 47-7 over Chicago, and, years later, Frank Gifford says, "I think that one game was the turning point for pro football." It drew nearly 57,000 at Yankee Stadium, blasting the air with a new chant, "Dee-fense! Dee-fense!" The '56 Giants were more than America's Team. They were New York's team when New York was America's Stage, when heroes were heroes and the Baby Boomers were gathering memories. If a ballplayer grabbed New York by the tail, the rest of the country stood up and saluted. Quarterback Charlie Conerly was the first Marlboro Man. Safety Jimmy Patton, symbolically larger than life, blew smoke from a Times Square billboard.

Long-suffering Giants fans remember them all. Gifford, Alex Webster, Mel Triplett, and Joe Morrison carrying the ball. Conerly, Don Heinrich, and Y.A. Tittle throwing it. Kyle Rote, Bob Schnelker, and Del Shofner catching it. Ben Agajanian, Pat Summerall, and Don Chandler kicking it. Patton, Emlen Tunnel, Dick Lynch, Dick Nolan, and Erich Barnes intercepting it. Stadium announcers didn't introduce defensive players in those days, but Ed Sullivan introduced the Giants. CBS telecast a documentary on "The Violent World of Sam Huff." Dick Modzelewski, Jim Katcavage, Rosey Grier, and Andy Robustelli were a fearsome foursome before most teams even used four defensive linemen. Of course, they didn't have to fight through blocks by Ray Wietecha, Darrell Dess, Jack Stroud, and Roosevelt Brown. And Jim Lee Howell's coaching staff included Vince Lombardi and Tom Landry.

In eight glorious years, the Giants played for six NFL championships. They won only the first time, in 1956, but they stole fans' hearts that weren't returned for 30 years.

The era ended December 29, 1963, at Chicago, with Tittle hobbling on a bad leg. The 14-10 defeat was created by an overpowering Bears defense. The next 17 years, the Giants went 84-156-4. They had two winning seasons, and even one of those was a cruel joke. The 1970 team went into its last game 9-4 with a chance for the playoffs before losing 31-3 to the Rams.

The team crumbled swiftly to 2-10-2 in 1964, under head coach Allie Sherman. The 1966 team was even worse. It gave up more than 50 points three times, set an NFL record by allowing 501, and finished 1-12-1. And by 1967, the common refrain sung at Giants games was, "Goodbye Allie."

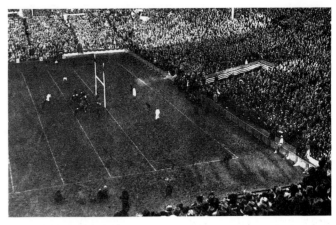

Pro football emerged from obscurity on December 6, 1925, when 73,000 fans crowded into the Polo Grounds (above) to watch the Giants play the Chicago Bears and their exciting star, Red Grange (left). The Bears beat the Giants 19-7, with Grange scoring once on an interception. More important than the score was the result: the positive reaction from the public and press saved the New York franchise. Nine years later (below), the Giants defeated the Bears 30-13 to win the 1934 NFL title in the famous "Sneakers Game." The Bears led 10-3 at halftime as the two teams slipped around on the frozen field. But the Giants came out for the third quarter wearing tennis shoes, and, led by Ed Danowski (22) and Ken Strong, they outscored the Bears 27-3 in the second half to win the championship.

From 1956 to 1963, the Giants tantalized their fans by playing for the NFL championship six times, but they won just once, 47-7 over the Bears in 1956. Kyle Rote (above left) boosted the 1956 score to 40-7 when he caught a nine-yard pass from Charlie Conerly. In the 1958 title game, called by many "the greatest ever played," Baltimore Colts fullback Alan Ameche (above right) scored on a one-yard run with 8:15 gone in overtime to frustrate the Giants 23-17. Y.A. Tittle led New York to three successive conference titles from 1961-63, but the Giants lost all three championship games. Particularly frustrating was 1963 (middle) when Tittle (14) was sacked by the Bears' Larry Morris (33) in the second quarter and strained a knee, hampering his play the rest of the way as the Giants lost 14-10. In the mid and late 1950s, the Giants assembled a remarkable coaching staff (below right), which included defensive coach Tom Landry (rear left), head coach Jim Lee Howell (center), end coach Ken Kavanaugh (rear right), offensive coach Vince Lombardi (front left), and line coach John Dell Isola (front right). Conerly (below left) quarterbacked the Giants to three conference titles and one NFL title.

Goodbye became an actuality after a 7-7 season in 1968.

The hated Jets won their Super Bowl following the 1968 season. Even worse, they beat the Giants 37-14 in a preseason game in 1969. Alex Webster had replaced Sherman through 1973, the 2-11-1 season that ended with the Giants' eviction from Yankee Stadium, which was scheduled for renovation. Then they had to play in the Yale Bowl, 77 miles from the city. Giants Stadium would not be ready until 1976.

From 1966 through 1974, none of the Giants' seven first-round draft choices lasted more than four seasons. Only two lasted that long (Jim Files and John Hicks). They tried eight starting quarterbacks from 1973 through 1980. Remember Jim Del Gaizo? Randy Dean? Jerry Golsteyn?

"By continuing to try for the quick fix, we were digging our own hole," owner Wellington Mara said, looking back. In 1974, the solution was to make Hall of Fame defensive end Andy Robustelli general manager after 10 years of running a travel agency, and to make Bill Arnsparger, Miami's two-time Super Bowl defensive genius, the head coach. Robustelli's five-year record of 21-51 appeared to bottom out with the 0-9 start of 1976, when John McVay succeeded Arnsparger, who was fired. "We were always finding different ways to lose," says Harry Carson, who was a rookie that year.

"That was the dark ages," says George Martin, a Giant since '75. "We were wandering in the wilderness. We were a pretty dismal group of men. We didn't look at being in the NFL as a profession. It was a six-month endeavor. We were football players. Today, we are professional athletes."

By 1978, the Giants had stopped drafting disappointments. They won five of their first eight games, and still had a chance for the playoffs when their sixth victory was one snap away in the twelfth game, November 19, 1978. They led 17-12, they had the ball, the clock showed 31 seconds, and the Eagles were out of time outs.

"In the huddle, I remember some confusion over what we were going to do," says Brad Benson, the only remaining Giant from that huddle. "I was only a second-year player, and I couldn't believe it. I still can't believe it."

Few people could believe their eyes when they saw quarterback Joe Pisarcik turn to give the ball to Larry Csonka instead of falling on it. The ball fell to the ground, and Eagles safety Herman Edwards picked it up. He took it 26 yards for the winning touchdown. "The most horrifying play in Giants history," McVay called it.

"It was a total, sheer embarrassment," Benson says.

The assistant coach who called the play was fired the next day. The Giants lost three of their next four games by a combined score of 81-37. Two weeks after the fumble, about 100 tickets were burned outside Giants Stadium. The ashes were mailed to Mara. The next week, before the last home game, eight fans contributed $375 for a plane to fly a banner over the stadium. It read, "15 Years of Lousy Football—We've Had Enough."

Wellington Mara was 9 when his father, Timothy J. Mara, founded the Giants in 1925. He remembers walking out of church and hearing his father tell some friends, "I'm going to try to put professional football over in New York today." In the 1930s, Timothy turned the team over to his sons Jack and Wellington, who ran it with brotherly love until Jack died in 1965. Jack's son Tim stayed uninvolved until the late 1970s, when it dawned on him that he was the one long-suffering Giants fan who could do something about the problems.

He started exercising his 50-percent ownership vote. On the matter of Robustelli's successor, the vote kept coming out in ties until Valentine's Day, 1979, when the Maras accepted Commissioner Pete Rozelle's recommendation of George Young, the personnel director at Miami. The Maras haven't

spoken since. But they have listened to Young, the silver lining in the 1978 cloudburst, who still hasn't seen film of that Eagles game.

"This all started with Ray Perkins," Carson said, days before Super Bowl XXI. "He laid the foundation. We were somewhat of a country club before he got here." Perkins ran the Giants through three-hour practices twice a day in training camp. He made football a full-time job. "Everybody began to believe in the program," Carson said.

It didn't happen right away. The 1980 Giants lost eight in a row after winning one. More tickets went up in flames. "That spoke to us, knowing how hard it is to get tickets in Giants Stadium," Martin says. But Taylor was drafted number-one the next year. And Rob Carpenter, who made enough third-and-2 plays for the offense to get the Giants into the playoffs, was picked up in a trade with Houston.

Looking back, Parcells, who was the defensive coordinator then, singles out the twelfth game in 1981. It was against Philadelphia, the same opponent in the twelfth game three years earlier. Again, the Giants were 5-6 after losing three straight. But this time, the Eagles were tough. They'd just been to the Super Bowl. They were 9-2. But this time the Giants won 20-10. "That was a start in the right direction," Parcells says. "Then we beat Dallas in overtime in the last game to get into the playoffs."

Perkins left to succeed the legendary Paul (Bear) Bryant as coach at the University of Alabama after 1982, the 4-5 strike season. Under Parcells, the Giants started 2-2 in 1983. Then it happened once more. They went 1-10-1 the rest of the way. Twenty-five players wound up on injured reserve. A home game against St. Louis, played in a severe rain storm, set an NFL record with 51,589 no-shows. The Giants lost 58 turnovers, a league high. They nearly lost Taylor, who signed with the USFL. Carson also wanted out.

It was a tragic period, too. Former running back Doug Kotar and assistant coach Bob Ledbetter died. Parcells's parents both died within six weeks. In recent years, the Giants probably have hung the most crepe in professional sports. Defensive tackle Troy Archer died in a car crash before the 1979 season. The 1986 Giants wore cornerback Carl (Spider) Lockhart's Number 43 on their chests and fullback John Tuggle's 38 on the back of their helmets. They died, like Kotar, of cancer, which also forced linebacker Dan Lloyd to retire early. Lloyd's poignant observation before Super Bowl XXI was, "I'd rather be watching the game on TV than have my number on everybody's jersey."

Three days after the 1983 season, Young met with Parcells. It was reported Young already had tried to hire University of Miami coach Howard Schnellenberger, his friend from Don Shula's staffs in Miami and Baltimore. But the next day, Young gave Parcells one more year.

If he had only one chance, Parcells wanted it to be a good one. He asked for and got a weight room and a strength coach. He made the drafting standards higher for size and speed. "I want to get these guys as big as you can without getting ridiculous," he told personnel director Tom Boisture.

The Giants' injured-reserve list dwindled to six players in Parker's first season. After three seasons, only two of the 35 regulars in his offseason program had missed games because of injuries, and there wasn't much a strength coach could do about Jim Burt's chronically bad back or the Astro-Turf seam that wrecked Zeke Mowatt's knee. "He made players look forward to weight training and all that lonely drudgery," said J.T. Turner, a guard in Parker's first offseason. Parcells called Parker "as valuable as any coach on this team, including myself."

The Giants didn't just grow healthier. They also grew bigger. The 1986 team was the NFL's biggest, averaging 231.2 pounds per man. Twelve of the

22 starters had changed from 1983, almost always to bigger players. Mark Bavaro was a 245-pound tight end instead of Tom Mullady at 232. Gary Reasons at 245 played inside linebacker instead of Brian Kelley at 222. Benson's body-by-Parker weighed 270 instead of 258. Carl Banks, relatively big at 235, was the smallest of the top seven linebackers by 10 pounds.

The next step was an offense. Carson remembers the 1983 AFC-NFC Pro Bowl, where the 49ers' Bill Walsh was the head coach. "The offense kept moving the ball up and down the field," he says, "and Lawrence and I kept looking at each other and saying, 'Must be nice to have an offense.' "

The Giants returned to the playoffs in 1984 without one. They could throw long, but nothing else. The fullback-oriented running game was one of two in the league that didn't produce a 30-yard run. They ranked twenty-second in rushing touchdowns and next-to-last in yards per carry. But in the second half of the season, Morris emerged as a dependable running back. The Giants just had to get the right people around him.

Young had been the first NFL general manager to sign a USFL player to a future contract, cornerback Kenny Daniel for 1984. Now, for 1985, he tapped the USFL for center Bart Oates and fullback Maurice Carthon. Guard Chris Godfrey already had come over in 1984. "You add three guys like that and you have an instant running game," Morris said. Punter Sean Landeta jumped leagues, too, and helped keep Morris away from his own goal line. Fred Hoaglin was hired as new offensive line coach.

The 1985 Giants added 50 rushing yards per game to their 1984 average. They leaped from twenty-second to fourth with 153 a game. They doubled their rushing touchdowns to 24. Morris had 21 himself, four on runs of more than 40 yards. The Giants were almost there.

That season ended January 5, 1986, with a 21-0 loss at Chicago. For the third year in five, the Giants had won the wild-card game but lost the next. This time was different, though. This time, as Bears head coach Mike Ditka said a year later, "Even though they lost the game, in effect they won."

They won the confidence that next time, they'd win the game. In the locker room, Parcells flat-out promised veterans Carson and Martin they'd be in the Super Bowl the next year. He told the other players they had "let these two classy gentlemen down." Carson spoke, too. He said he wouldn't even think about retiring with the Giants so close to winning it all. "I told them I didn't want to be close next year," Carson recalled. "I wanted the whole thing."

The Giants started talking about Super Bowl XXI as if they'd made reservations. An air of inevitability developed. That wasn't enough, of course. The Rams had made it one round past the Giants in 1985, and they were pretty sure they were a year away from the Super Bowl, too. The main lesson from the loss at Chicago, Simms said, was "the intensity level they played at was extremely high. We always thought we were an intense team, and we found out from them we had to step it up just one more notch."

The confidence took some dings in training camp. With one preseason game left, someone asked Parcells if the team was as far along as he'd hoped. "Nope," he said.

Placekicks still were an adventure. The Giants would go through six kickers in two years. But Raul Allegre locked the revolving door. He made the difference in four consecutive midseason games.

Fullback George Adams would miss the season with a chipped femur. He had led Giants backs in catches in 1985 as a rookie. But Bavaro and veteran running back Tony Galbreath picked up the slack. Defensive left end Curtis McGriff would miss the season with a hamstring injury. Martin hadn't played regularly for five years. But he did now, and he played well.

Morris held out most of training camp, signing only hours before the opening kickoff. But whenever the passing game fluttered, Morris carried the team.

Things got a little dicey after the Giants blew a late lead at Dallas and lost the season-opening game 31-28. These defensive letdowns were getting out of hand. The 1985 Giants actually lost three of the five times they scored more than 28 points. Parcells went to Martin and Carson. "I got on them and they got on their teammates," he said.

It didn't happen again. The Giants lost only once more. They won their last 12.

"Not only did we have to overcome the people we played for sixteen games and the playoffs, but there was a lot of history involved," Oates said. "There's a long history of losing in this organization, and we were able to overcome all that losing by overcoming choking in the big game."

The Giants learned how to win. They learned to take advantage of their breaks. Then they learned to look for chances to *make* their breaks. They learned to make key plays and avoid key mistakes. They learned they could still win if they fell behind. They learned they could hold on to late leads.

"I think the major difference between winning and almost winning is mental," Benson said. "Attitude counts for a lot, especially when you go into a game just *knowing* you're the better team."

It made the difference between losing six games by 20 points in 1985 and winning six consecutive games by a total of 22 points in 1986. The Giants' record went from 3-6 to 9-2 in games decided by seven points or less, 1-4 to 5-1 in games decided by three or less. They won games at Minnesota and San Francisco they had no business winning. "It seems like it's someone different every week," Carson said. "Everyone feels we're going to make the big play."

They took some big chances. You can't reach for the Super Bowl with your arms folded. The Giants made 10 of their 14 tries on fourth down, including eight of their last nine. "The old Giants were content to keep games close," guard Billy Ard said. "This year, we've been going for it and getting it." Against Minnesota, Denver, and San Francisco in games 10 through 12, fourth-down plays made the eventual difference.

Minnesota was the big one. The Giants trailed 20-19 with 1:12 to play. It was fourth-and-17 from their 48, but they had to go for it. Bobby Johnson's 22-yard catch kept the winning drive alive. "If we had lost that game, I think we'd have been pretty down," Johnson said later. Parcells called it "the most important play of the season."

The next two weeks, the Giants could have punted on fourth down. But a run from punt formation led to the first field goal when they beat Denver 19-16. And Morris's fourth-and-2 run, after Parcells had waved the offense back onto the field, resurrected the second scoring drive in the comeback at San Francisco. The Giants' 21 points in nine minutes overcame a 17-0 halftime deficit. Their air of inevitability started catching on. "Did you see that?" Banks said after the game. "I couldn't believe it was happening myself."

The passing game fell together just in time. For the first 12 games, Simms had a 70.5 rating. He took 3.3 sacks a game. He threw 13 touchdown passes and 16 interceptions. In the last seven games, his rating was 104.9. He took 1.5 sacks a game and threw 16 touchdowns and 6 interceptions. He was NFL player of the month in December.

This was getting to be fun. Parcells had joked about the burden of high expectations back in April, when the NFC East coaches picked the Giants to win the division. How did he feel about that? "About how I feel about going to lunch in Tripoli," he said. But it was better than being expected to trip

From 1964 through 1980, the Giants won 84 games, lost 156, and tied 4. Even Fran Tarkenton (right in photograph at far left) couldn't keep coach Allie Sherman from being fired. Running back Rocky Thompson (right), the Giants' number-one draft choice in 1971, lasted just three years. He was one of seven first-round draft choices in a nine-year period who didn't play longer than four years with the team.

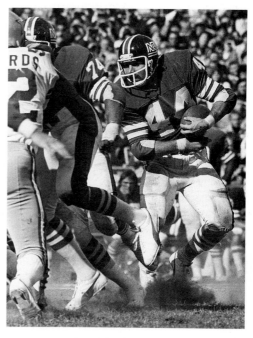

Captains from the Giants and New York Jets (middle left) said hello in 1974, the second year the Giants played at the Yale Bowl; they produced a humbling 2-12 record. Sure enough, the Giants lost to the Jets, too, 26-20 in overtime. Running back Doug Kotar (above right in a 1975 photo) was one of several New York players to die of cancer in recent years. Left: In 1975, seven of the great names in Giants history gathered for this photograph. They included (back row, left to right) Andy Robustelli, Tom Landry, Wellington Mara, and Dick Nolan, and (front row) Frank Gifford, Sam Huff, and Harland Svare.

over any bump in the schedule. "We proved ourselves when people had only bad things to say about us," Benson said, "so having to prove ourselves now that everybody loves us isn't that different."

The defense always had been the strength of the Giants, all the way back to the 1950s. Now, with their big, fast linebackers, it seemed as if they were using 12 players. "They're the only team in football that doesn't need a safety to help force on runs," Redskins defensive coordinator Richie Petitbon said. "They stop runs with seven guys, not eight. The safety can sit back there and never be out of position if you pass instead of run."

Pass rushes worked the same way. Most teams have to send five or six men to make a quarterback panic. The Giants did it with four, usually three linemen and Taylor. For the most part, Taylor was a lineman, too. He stood up, but he rushed the passer 85 percent of the time in 1986, twice his rate of the previous year. Why waste the guy in coverage when he could get past two blockers and still hassle the quarterback?

The Giants' four-man gang of pass rushers let them play more zone defense than most teams that give quarterbacks nightmares. There's an extra man for coverage. About 80 percent of the time, the Giants leave two safeties deep.

In theory, zone coverage gives receivers more room to get open. The defenders cover general areas, not specific men. But when a pass play begins, the defenders still are close together. The Giants' pass rush makes the quarterback unload the ball before the defenders spread out. The receivers don't have much open space. "They force you to change your timing," Denver wide receiver Steve Watson said.

When someone asked Dallas quarterback Danny White what was so tough about the Giants' defense, he said, "That's like saying, 'What's so good about chocolate cake?' I always felt that their strength is that they have no weakness. They have a tremendous knack for covering the field and pressuring the quarterback. Normally, you expect one thing or another."

They weren't tricky. The main way the Giants messed with a quarterback's mind was by thumping his helmet. Most of the top defenses could stuff mattresses with all their formations and coverage diagrams, but the Giants prided themselves in being simple. "We don't get into trying to keep up with the Joneses," Banks said.

They didn't have to. "They line up and say, 'We're going to come at you. Try to knock us off the ball,' " Denver center Billy Bryan said. "Their front seven is the strongest I can remember playing against."

The Giants got a lot of notoriety for knocking eight quarterbacks out of games in two seasons. They even had a three-game streak of White, Philadelphia's Ron Jaworski, and Minnesota's Tommy Kramer in 1986, and the two-season count probably would have been nine if Washington had gotten the ball back once more in the NFC Championship Game. But they didn't intimidate teams as much as they frustrated them. They gave up the third-most pass completions in the league, but for the third-lowest gain per catch. All they gave up were short passes, and it takes a lot of short ones to reach the end zone.

They went by the book. Stop the run, anticipate the pass, deck the passer. It's a logical progression, and the Giants made the dominos fall especially hard in their last six games, when no opponent even tried more than 20 running plays. They led the league by allowing 80.3 rushing yards per game in the regular season, then virtually halved that to 40.3 in three playoff games.

The mastermind of this defense is Bill Belichick, a former 170-pound lineman from Wesleyan College in Connecticut. "He's thirty-four years old,

but his head is fifty," Parcells says. Belichick always has been a coach. When he was 10, he watched film with his father, Steve, an assistant at Navy. He doodled with X's and O's when he was supposed to be doing homework. When he was out of college in 1975, he took a $25-a-week job with Baltimore Colts head coach Ted Marchibroda just so he could pick his brain on the one-hour drives to and from work.

"He was like a blotter," Marchibroda said. "He absorbed everything. If you gave him something, he came back with a little more." He caught on so quickly, Parcells made him his successor as defensive coordinator in 1983, Belichick's fifth season with the Giants. But as the latest hot assistant coach at the Super Bowl circus, Belichick hid his meteor under a basket.

The Giants are like that. "We don't have the 'Super Bowl Shuffle' here," Oates says. "We may be boring from a Fifth Avenue standpoint, but what we have here fits perfectly."

The celebration after the NFC Championship Game had all the rowdiness of a real-estate closing. Oates said it was "very, very satisfying, but still just another day at the office." All season, they went from one game to another, all but calling out "Next!" like a butcher. Even the party after Super Bowl XXI was more of a wide grin than a big blast. "That's how Bill Parcells has made this team," starting strong safety Kenny Hill said. "When I won with the Raiders, it was wild. But this team is essentially emotionless."

New York certainly plays with emotion. "When I first came to the Giants, that's one thing they did not have here—enthusiasm for big plays," says Taylor, who makes a point of jumping on any defensive teammate who scores. But the enthusiasm is limited to plays on the field. The Giants don't go jockeying for headlines or endorsements. They don't bark at opponents on the field or brag on themselves off of it. They carry their lunch pails to work and roll up their sleeves.

"The Giants are good because they play as a team," Ditka says. "They don't give a damn who gets the credit." They don't even give out game balls.

"We don't have characters," Benson says. "We have family men." They go home and pet their dogs, not kick them. Throwing Gatorade on their coach is their only eccentric indulgence.

That ritual actually started in 1984, and Jim Burt was the first to douse Parcells. The coach had goaded him all week. Burt was only trying to get even, not get attention. But as the barrel was passed to Carson, and the victories became weekly, Parcells's shower became the victory cigar Giants' fans looked forward to.

Even in the bad and booing days, Martin says, "Giants fans always looked at us like family. They'd criticize us, but it was never all right for anyone else to." Now, if Madison Avenue finds the players dull in their success, that's fine with the long-suffering. They didn't wait all these years to have someone yank the players from their embrace to sell motorcycles.

"I never thought I'd see this in my lifetime," Bert Mollar, a 31-year-old fan, told a reporter after the Super Bowl. He was in one of the city's many drinking establishments where high spirits flowed. "I mean, we are talking the Sahara Desert of football teams. I feel like I've found an oasis." The players felt the same way. As Carson put it, "For so many years, to think we would win a Super Bowl would be to question our sanity."

But now, New York was crazy with ecstasy. The Empire State Building dressed its top floors in red, white, and blue lights, the Giants' colors. Wellington Mara was accepting the Lombardi Trophy. He thought, "Gosh this thing's heavy. I sure hope I don't drop it." Not a chance. Not this year. In 1986, everything the Giants touched went up in dreams.

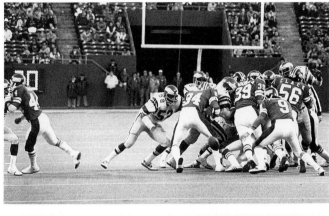

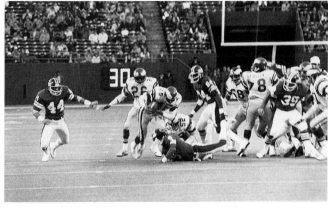

Head coach John McVay called it "the most horrifying play in Giants history." Leading 17-12 with 31 seconds remaining in a 1978 game with Philadelphia, the Giants ran a play, instead of having quarterback Joe Pisarcik fall on the ball. But Larry Csonka (39), who took a handoff from Pisarcik, fumbled (above left), and Eagles safety Herman Edwards (46, above right) scooped up the ball. While the Giants watched in shock, Edwards ran 26 yards for the winning touchdown.

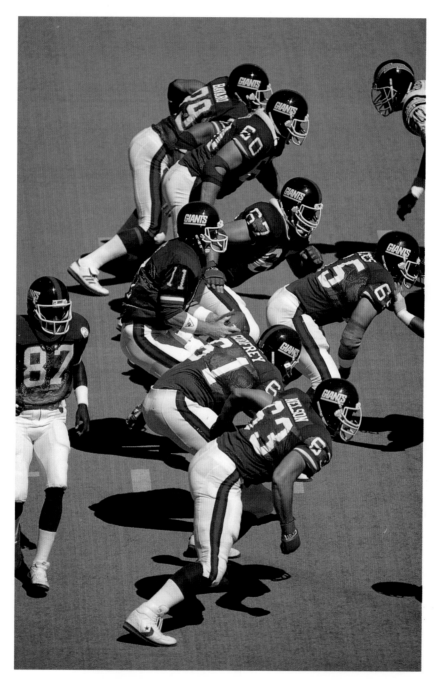

The Giants' offensive line—tight end Mark Bavaro (89), left tackle Brad Benson (60), left guard Billy Ard (67), center Bart Oates (65), right guard Chris Godfrey (61), and right tackle Karl Nelson (63) —provided quarterback Phil Simms (11) a wall of protection.

Simms (left) earned Super Bowl XXI most-valuable-player honors one year after receiving the AFC-NFC Pro Bowl player-of-the-game award in 1986.

Street-tough Bavaro (above) set a Giants record for most receptions by a tight end with 66, good for 1,001 yards.

Joe Morris, "Little Joe" to New York fans, broke his own team record with 1,516 yards rushing during the 1986 regular season.

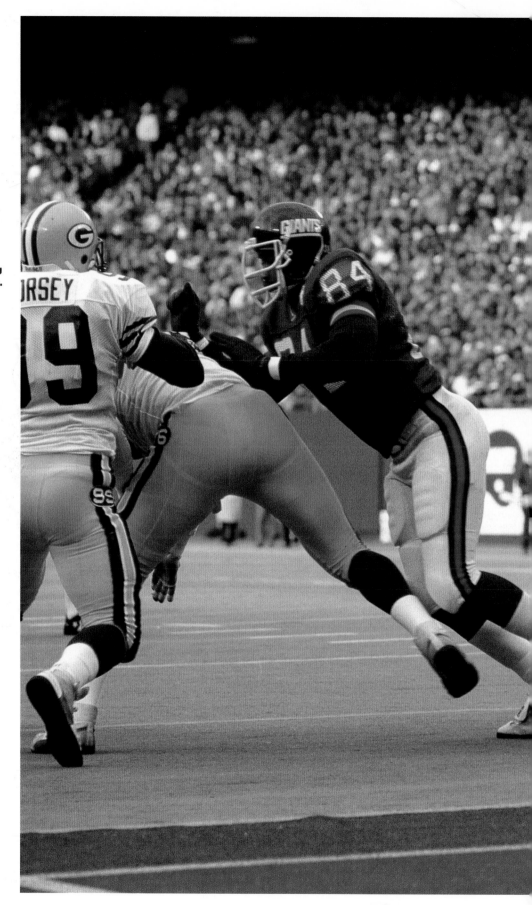

Quick and deadly Lionel Manuel (left) missed most of the season with a hyperextended knee, but returned in time to help the New York passing game in three impressive playoff victories.

Tackle Benson (above), the anchor of the Giants' offensive line, and the only offensive lineman ever to be named an NFC player of the week, deserved his selection to the NFC Pro Bowl team.

The Giants' defense was the toughest against the run in the NFL in 1986, thanks to the play of linebackers Carl Banks (58) and Harry Carson (53) and nose tackle Jim Burt (64).

Defensive left end George Martin (right) broke open the regular season game against Denver with a 78-yard interception return for a touchdown.

In 1986, running into the center of the Giants' defense was no place for any opposing player with a weak heart — or body.

Linebacker Lawrence Taylor, the NFL's pass-rusher supreme, led the league with 20.5 quarterback sacks in 1986.

Leonard Marshall (left), who lined up in front of Taylor, and some fancy stunting, helped give the Giants the best one-two sack combination in the NFL in 1986. Marshall had 12.

Andy Headen (54, above), here with Martin putting pressure on San Diego quarterback Dan Fouts, added to the Giants' exceptional linebacking rotation.

Carson (left), an 11-year veteran who has played in eight Pro Bowls, was the team captain and emotional leader of New York's defense.

Bill Parcells, the Giants' coach since 1983, has developed his team into the NFL's best.

31

Using Gatorade instead of the
traditional champagne, Carson
gave Parcells the Giants' ver-
sion of the victory shower.

THE MEN

*FROM PARCELLS
THROUGH TAYLOR*

BILL PARCELLS
H e a d   C o a c h

Bill Parcells is the kind of coach who can calm down a nervous young receiver on the sideline. "Don't worry about doing everything perfect now," NFL Films caught him telling Stacy Robinson. "Just go out there and run like hell and catch it. You know what I mean? Like a street game."

Parcells also is the kind of coach who can rile up an offensive line for a playoff game. "Club 13," he called the Giants' linemen before they played San Francisco in the divisional playoffs. He made it hard for them to forget that New York had a total of only 13 rushing yards in the regular-season game against the 49ers. "We could have done better than that running thirteen quarterback sneaks," he told them. Then, the day after the Giants ran for 216 yards in winning the rematch 49-3, Parcells told guard Chris Godfrey, "I'm not all that happy with what the line did yesterday," and said to pass the word.

"He has this incredible feel for what people need," Phil McConkey says. "He pushes all the right buttons. They call Reagan the Great Communicator, but Bill could have the same nickname. Different people have to be treated in different ways, and Bill has learned how to get through to each one of us."

He doesn't want robots, Parcells says. He wants players. People. He tries to talk to each player each day. "He's more or less one of us," says Harry Carson, the defensive captain. "He's a players-type coach."

Parcells knows when to let Leonard Marshall bow to the crowd after sacking the quarterback in practice.

He knows when to lay into Jim Burt or Brad Benson, Pro Bowl players with free-agent physical gifts. They may not like it, but, as Benson says, "I was on my way out of here, but he took a chance on me. He's afraid if he tells me I'm doing a good job, I'll slack off."

He knows when to put his arm around Lawrence Taylor and point the way to an addiction rehab center. "Bill helped me more than anyone else," Taylor said. "I have to thank him for giving me strength."

He knows when to hug them, he knows when to slug them, and he knows when to call a fake punt that turns the Super Bowl around. He knows when to let big kids act like little kids and dump gallons of sticky, cold drink on his head.

Parcells can keep his dignity, even dripping wet. Maybe it's because he never had the look of a dynamic leader in the first place. He doesn't have Shula's stare or Landry's laurels or Walsh's waistline. He doesn't inspire drumrolls or deep-voiced awe. All he has is respect, and not even a victory shower of Gatorade washes that away.

"He has enough security in himself as a coach," Benson says, "to know he can allow that in the closing seconds of a game and know he can have control when the game is over and he talks to us in the meeting room."

He doesn't even hide his superstitions. "My mother had quite an array that served us well," he says. Going to work, he drinks three cups of coffee at the same places every morning. He opens his locker with the heads-up penny on the floor, then goes to his office with the herd of elephant figurines, all trunks up. He has made good-luck charms of a truck driver who talked his way into a practice and a pilot who had flown two champions to their Super Bowls.

That pilot, Augie Stasio, flew the Giants to Pasadena. Even Carson is a rabbit's foot, always at Parcells's left for the National Anthem, team pictures, and bus rides. "Just because you're superstitious doesn't mean you're a loony bird," Parcells says.

No one calls him a genius, either. His players call him Tuna.

"Because he's big and fat like a tuna," says Carson, who likes to point out a fat spectator as practice winds down and ask Parcells if it's his brother.

"I love kidding around with them," Parcells says. "It makes me feel twenty-five years old. You'll go crazy in this business if you don't laugh once in a while."

He jokes about his weight, too. He said he lost six pounds Super Bowl week, but it was "like throwing a deck chair off the Queen Mary." Diets? Parcells tries diets. He says he stops eating dessert after breakfast.

"I'll get Harry," he says of Carson, the dumper of the Gatorade. "I'm half Italian, and we're famous for two things: spaghetti and revenge."

There's a difference between taking his job seriously and taking himself seriously. If someone wants to take Parcells too seriously, make a big hoo-ha because he's Coach of the Year, he'll brush them off like incense peddlers at the airport.

"Hey, I'm just like anybody else," he says. "I'm just a guy." A lucky guy, he admits. He's had the success he wants in the job he wants, just 12 miles from his North Jersey hometown, Oradell. But a great coach? "All them guys that are great coaches," he says, "it's because they've got really good players."

He knows there are good coaches no one ever heard of, working places where they have to line the fields before practice and wash the uniforms after practice. He knows because he did that at Hastings College in Nebraska. His first coaching job was there. He tried to win then.

He tries to win now. Coaching at Hastings isn't all that different from coaching in the Super Bowl.

In fact, as the victory over Denver ended, that's what Parcells thought about, his first game at Hastings in 1964.

His team beat the Colorado School of Mines. The score was 24-0. "It was important at the time," he said.

He knows there are good coaches who lose. "A lot of coaches may be perceived as failures because they didn't have enough time," he says. "Unfortunately, in this league—and it didn't used to be that way in sports—you're judged by winning. If you win, you get to stay."

Parcells almost didn't get to stay after his first year as the Giants' head coach in 1983. They went 3-12-1. After four years of Ray Perkins's mirthless militarism, players were seeking asylum in the trainer's room. The price of success was going unpaid. Parcells had to pop for the interest.

Only 11 players from the 1982 squad went to Super Bowl XXI. The purge left the Giants with Parcells's kind of guys playing Parcells's kind of football. They wore work shirts, not gold chains. They wore industrial boots, not alligator shoes.

They wore the other teams out. The Big Blue Wrecking Crew put in an honest day's work, rolling victories off the assembly line.

Parcells's kind of football leaves dirt under the nails. He was a defensive assistant for 17 years, remember. He sneers at "fancy quarterbacks strutting around and dancing on the field," at "little wide receivers who run like the wind, who probably can't take a major-league hit." He says, "This is the part of the country where guys are tough, where teams have to be tough and mean and straight ahead."

It's like this: They run the ball. They throw when they have to, but they run the ball. And they play defense. Not fancy. Not complicated. Just tough, hard-nosed defense.

Everybody tackles the guy with the ball, and they let him know they'll be back to tackle him again.

He calls his kind of players "lunch-pail guys." They're not necessarily better athletes. They just do "all they can do all the time." He can't test for lunch pails at the scouting workouts, but he'll talk to a prospect for eight hours, searching. If the kid can carry a metaphorical lunch pail, Parcells will work with him.

He'll laugh with him, scream at him, win with him.

"We don't see him as just a head coach," George Martin says. "We see him as a friend who's the boss."

GEORGE YOUNG
General Manager

When George Young joined the Giants, they had gone seven years without a winning season. Their owners didn't speak to each other. Giants tickets had become kindling. The word "hopeless" found its way into his first press conference.

Hopeless? Not at all, Young said. Why, look at the way Konrad Adenauer brought Germany back from World War II. Konrad who? The Giants needed a rib-rocking, jaw-jutting savior, and here was this pleasant, plump man giving a history lesson. He *was* a teacher. He had taught high school history for 15 years in Baltimore's inner city. He had master's degrees in educational administration and history/political science. He knew his way around a reference library.

But he knew how to read a playbook, too. Young was a football man. He had been a Little All-America tackle at Bucknell in 1951, and he had coached two under-funded high schools into juggernauts, winning six state championships. More to the point, Young had been coaching and scouting in the NFL since 1968, when he was 37. He was the guy Don Shula entrusted to run his front office in Miami.

For a team that couldn't even fall on the ball to win a game, maybe it wasn't a bad idea to hire someone smart enough to earn two master's degrees. A few years later, Young would pull a doozy on the USFL's Baltimore Stars. They allowed center Bart Oates to shop for NFL offers, but they retained the right to match anything he found. Young wanted Oates, so he included a bonus of $1.1 million in the contract if his league—the NFL—folded. It was no risk for an NFL team, but a dangerous clause for a USFL team to match.

Few teams scouted the USFL more thoroughly, or harvested its players more effectively. "I always subscribed to the sponge theory," Young said. "You immerse yourself in a subject and soak up as much knowledge as you can." Young signed little-known USFL free agents—Oates, guard Chris Godfrey, fullback Maurice Carthon, and punter Sean Landeta—because he needed run blockers more than headliners. He drafted tackle Gary Zimmerman, too, and when Zimmerman balked at playing in the East, he traded him to Minnesota for two second-round choices.

When he was coaching high schools, Young became known around the NFL because he went to every coaching clinic within 100 miles. Baltimore Colts head coaches Weeb Ewbank and Shula had him out to camp to talk football. After the 1967 season, Young was the man Shula called when he needed help scouting film of draft prospects. He liked Young's reports so much, he offered him a full-time scouting job.

"My friends thought I was crazy," Young said of taking the job. There's no tenure in pro football, they told him. But Young figured Shula never would have to scrap for work, and he was ready for a new challenge. In the next 11 years, including five with Miami, he was a personnel director, offensive line coach, offensive coordinator, and Shula's right-hand man.

In New York, Young said, "My first order of business was to build the team's self-respect." He reminded people of its proud tradition. He wore his ring from the Colts' Super Bowl V victory for one year, "to give people the idea it was a very nice thing to have." But then he took it off and waited with the rest of them.

Self-respect would require better leadership and better players. Young had known Ray Perkins as a Colts receiver, and he had seen him several years later as an assistant coach scouting a college all-star game. Perkins spent the week watching every practice drill, while other coaches scouted the hotel pool. "Here's a guy after my own heart," Young said after he hired Perkins.

Young's first NFL draft selection was quarterback Phil Simms, a choice criticized by the Giants' fans and media. It was an odd choice, especially for an ex-lineman, to go for the flair before the foundation. "Why a quarterback?" Young said later. "Because that's where you start." He had seen Ewbank start his championship teams with John Unitas and Joe Namath. "The quarterback is your foundation. He's the guy who lets you sleep at night."

In Young's eight seasons, the Giants have put 15 players on all-rookie teams. He didn't doze after the first few rounds, either. NFC Pro Bowl nose tackle Jim Burt was an overlooked free agent. So were cornerback Elvis Patterson and wide receiver Bobby Johnson. The Giants took safety Herb Welch in the twelfth round, guard Billy Ard in the eighth, and cornerback Perry Williams and wide receiver Lionel Manuel in the seventh. They all started in the Super Bowl.

The fans were ready to put palm branches at Young's feet in 1981. After 17 years, the Giants made the playoffs. But Young knew they hadn't arrived. "We've shown progress, that's all," he said. "You can't speed up the rebuilding process." It would take detours. Perkins left. First-round star Mark Haynes and second-round choice Earnest Gray departed. The battered 1983 team needed reservations to get into the trainer's room. But Young remained patient.

After his first five teams went 26-46-1, his sixth returned to the playoffs. Young was NFL executive of the year in 1984. His last three teams are 33-15. But he's still not taking bows. "I'm one small facet of what's going on," he says.

RAUL ALLEGRE
Placekicker

SEAN LANDETA
Punter

Some Giants coaches got together for a golf game a few months after the 1985 season. No football talk, they agreed. They almost made it, too. They were on the sixteenth tee when offensive coordinator Ron Erhardt interrupted his swing, turned to the others, and said, "How the hell did he miss that punt?"

Sometimes, Sean Landeta thinks he could average 50 yards for 20 years, and his epitaph still would read, "Here Lies A Punter Who Missed The Ball."

Landeta didn't quite miss it. He nicked it. The play officially was a five-yard punt return, and it gave Chicago a 7-0 lead in the NFC Divisional Playoff Game it went on to win 21-0.

"I consider it just one of those freak things that happens once in a lifetime," Landeta says. Lord knows, he can kick in bad wind. The gusts in the NFC championship victory over Washington last January might as well have been a whisper, to look at Landeta's 43.3-yard average. But Chicago was just as blustery that day in 1985, winds gusting to 30 miles an hour, and Landeta says the ball moved two feet sideways between his hands and his foot.

"All I know is when I brought my leg forward, the ball wasn't in front of me anymore," he says. "I barely touched it."

At least he got noticed. People wrote stories about Landeta nearly everywhere the Giants went the next season. And they also mentioned that he led all NFC punters. His 44.8-yard average, second-best in the league, earned him a trip to Hawaii for the AFC-NFC Pro Bowl.

Before Super Bowl XXI, Bill Parcells called Landeta "directly responsible" for three regular-season victories. When the Giants beat the Raiders 14-9, Landeta's 55-yard punt to the 14 put the Raiders in a hole that eventually led to a 50-yard drive that put New York ahead 7-6. When they beat St. Louis 13-6, his nine punts averaged 47.9 yards and put the Cardinals inside their own 20 three times. When they beat Denver 19-16, his 48.8-yard average gave the Giants an average edge of 14 yards per exchange.

And in the NFC Championship Game, he didn't give back the 10 quick points the Giants got after short Washington punts into the wind.

The Giants could take Landeta's punting for granted, but it wasn't always that way with field goals. They couldn't even take their place-kicker's *name* for granted until Raul Allegre became their sixth kicker in 19 games, four weeks into the 1986 season.

Allegre made the difference in his first game, 20-17 over New Orleans, and then four in a row later on. He beat Minnesota and Denver in the final seconds.

The night before the Minnesota game, Allegre's seventh with the Giants, linebacker Gary Reasons saw him alone in the hotel coffee shop and invited him to join some other Giants. Allegre politely declined. He said he wasn't really part of the team yet.

"I felt like I was on a great team, but I was just going along for the ride," he said later. "I wanted to be able to do something. After that game, I knew I had a lot to do with a win."

When Reasons told Parcells the story, the coach gave Allegre the only game ball the Giants awarded all year.

Allegre had made the AFC Pro Bowl team as a rookie with the Baltimore Colts in 1983, when his 30-for-35 field-goal successes included 4 for 5 from 50 yards or more. Owner Robert Irsay rewarded him with a contract that paid $4,000 for each field goal and $1,000 for each extra point—on top of his salary. But the Colts cut him before the 1986 season.

The Giants tried him out 11 days later. Allegre made all 18 field-goal attempts, including one from 57 yards. He already had his name on a locker when Parcells, disgusted that the afternoon dragged on without a contract, kicked him out of the Giants' offices. Allegre hadn't been hard-lining for money, he said. In a letter to Parcells, he explained that he'd only been trying to understand his new contract.

Parcells called him back. In the Giants' fourth game, Allegre was their third placekicker.

Through the Super Bowl, he was 19 for 20 inside 40 yards, 7 for 12 from 41 through 47, and 26 for 34 altogether. "Kicking is confidence," he said. "If you feel you are going to make it, it works for you. I prepare for pressure every week."

Allegre had found kicking easy the first time he tried it. He was a soccer player from Torreon, Mexico, learning English as an 18-year-old high school senior in Sheldon, Washington. Landeta was the same age when he joined his high school team in Baltimore.

Landeta went on to lead Division II punters for Towson State in Baltimore, then played with the USFL's Philadelphia-Baltimore Stars in 1983-85. He averaged more than 42 yards in two of the Stars' three championship games, and the Giants snapped him up. He made all-rookie teams in 1985 despite having played a wearying 42 games in 52 weeks. In 1986, Landeta put 24 of 79 punts inside the 20, with only 11 touchbacks. His 37.1-yard net average ranked third in the NFL. Landeta gave each punt-squad player $100 for helping him get to Honolulu in February.

As Allegre said, "In pro football, kickers' lives go up and down like a football does."

Raul Allegre found a home as the Giants' placekicker.

Sean Landeta's punts played a key role in Giants victories.

CARL BANKS
L i n e b a c k e r

The Giants had the third pick in the 1984 draft. They had it on merit. They'd just finished 3-12-1. The USFL already had watered down the draft class like stew when company arrives, but the Giants couldn't be picky. They could use help almost anywhere. They had scored fewer points than all but three NFL teams. Their offense was truly offensive. Their one solid position was linebacker, where Harry Carson and Lawrence Taylor had gone to the last three AFC-NFC Pro Bowls and Brad Van Pelt had gone to five before that.

So what did they draft? A linebacker.

Bill Parcells didn't apologize. He had seen this linebacker, Carl Banks. At the Senior Bowl, Parcells said, "I spent six or seven minutes looking at him and never looked at him again. What's the use, unless you wanted to drool? Some things are obvious to you."

Banks obviously was going to be a great player. You can't get enough of those, even at one position. Van Pelt was 33. He had been Banks's childhood hero as a kid, long before Banks followed him to Michigan State. Van Pelt's best days were behind him when the Giants shipped him to the Vikings that year.

"I remember it," Banks said three seasons later. "Everybody was saying, 'Sure, he's a good player, but where's he going to play?' It was kind of hard to hear. You're a first-round draft pick, but people keep talking you down. But I knew I'd fit in."

Banks actually was looking forward to joining all those great linebackers. His friends couldn't believe it. They were wondering where he was going to play, too. To Banks, though, "It was a chance to learn from some of the best. I didn't say, 'I don't want to go there because I'll never be a star.' I figured I was better off learning from guys like L.T. and Harry. If I had gone somewhere else and they had just turned me loose, I wouldn't be as good a player as I am now."

Banks learned one thing from the start. "The tempo they set," he says. "When you're playing next to them, you've got to turn it up a notch." Not that Banks hadn't been cranked up in college. After one defeat, he broke a helmet in half. Another time, when Michigan State lost on a late flea-flicker, he said, "I just laid on the turf in front of 80,000 people and cried." This was a man who wanted to win.

He was willing to work at being a star, too. He didn't just watch Taylor with his eyes popping and his jaw hanging. He studied Taylor's footwork. He learned. Even now, he says, after a good game, "What I think about are not the plays I made, but the plays I *could* have made."

There was much Banks needed to learn at first. He had been main-

ly a run-stuffer in college. Another idol was Jack Ham, the Pittsburgh linebacker who may have been the NFL's best ever at pass coverage, but the thing that impressed Banks about Ham was the way this guy who weighed less than 220 pounds could knock tight ends back into a ball carrier's face.

In his first two seasons, Banks seldom played on passing downs. He shared the left outside linebacker job with Byron Hunt. He made all-rookie teams, even had a 10-tackle game with two sacks and a fumble recovery in his first start. But he started only four games in 1984 and five the next year, when he missed four altogether with a sprained knee.

In his third year, Banks was ready. He showed that in the first game, when he stopped Dallas's Tony Dorsett for two losses in the first quarter. Banks finally was using his instincts instead of thinking before he moved. He felt comfortable. "And when I'm comfortable out there, look out," he said.

Banks led the Giants with 120 tackles. Thirteen of them stopped runs behind the line. He ranked third on the team in sacks with 6½, and he hurried quarterbacks two more times. Banks played opposite Taylor, and George Martin said, "Carl has added balance to our defense. Whereas before, we had a lot of dominant ball players predominantly on our right side, Carl has balanced that up." If an offense got too preoccupied with keeping Taylor off the quarterback's shoulders, Banks was there on the other side to do the job just as well.

It wasn't until the playoffs that the rest of the nation noticed Banks. He led the team with a total of 26 tackles in three postseason games, all but three of them solos. He forced a hurried interception before the San Francisco game became a rout, and helped dissuade the 49ers from running by dumping tight end Russ Francis into the backfield, just the way he'd seen Ham do it. "Carl was a man with a mission," Leonard Marshall said.

Banks gave Washington more of the same the next week. Taylor missed much of the game with a leg injury, so Banks was the guy who made sure quarterback Jay Schroeder had a chaperone all day. In the Super Bowl, one of his team-high 10 solo tackles came the play before Rich Karlis missed his chip-shot field goal.

All that was too late for the Pro Bowl voters. Banks stayed home. But Denver head coach Dan Reeves said he might be the Giants' best linebacker, and that included you-know-who. "I'm very flattered," Banks said, "but there's only one Lawrence Taylor."

Taylor himself wasn't so sure of that. "I'm so proud of him," he said. "Every time you see him play, you say, 'Someone's got to be kidding that this guy didn't make all-pro.'"

MARK BAVARO
T i g h t   E n d

Mark Bavaro once played with a broken jaw wired shut for five weeks. "Not that anyone noticed," he said. A marble statue may have more to say than Bavaro. But then, it's not quite as solid.

"When you start rating guys on toughness," Harry Carson says, "put Mark Bavaro at the top of the list."

He chipped two teeth in the Giants' 1986 game against New Orleans. He had to have his jaw X-rayed. That was before he made five of his seven catches in the victory, six for first downs.

As a high school junior, he dislocated an elbow. "We figured he'd be out five, six weeks," said his coach, Ernie Smith. "He was back after two."

"When the pain gets too much, I don't play," Bavaro says. "Sometimes, it doesn't reach that point."

He probably wouldn't have lasted into the fourth round of the 1985 draft if he hadn't played with knee and shoulder injuries. Tim Rooney, the Giants' director of pro personnel, wasn't even scouting Bavaro when he discovered him. He was looking at film of Pittsburgh linebacker Chris Doleman, and the Notre Dame tight end kept beating up on his prospect.

The Giants knew they had a big-time blocker in Bavaro's first week at training camp. He was one-on-one with a linebacker, and tight end coach Mike Pope said, "There was a tremendous collision, like when a tackle and defensive end meet. He knocked the guy five, six yards off the line of scrimmage."

Not many tight ends can do that. It's hard to find the hybrid tackle-wide receiver that coaches want for the position. That's like crossing a rhino with a deer. In the NFL, with its increasing fascination for speed, tight ends tend to look more like deer. But they usually don't gain 1,000 yards receiving, as Bavaro did in his second season.

"I thought I coached the best blocking tight end," former Raiders coach John Madden said of Dave Casper, "but now I'm not sure." Madden had just seen Bavaro help the Giants beat Washington in the decisive game for the NFC East title, and he called it, "the greatest job of any tight end I've ever seen."

"He plays the position the way it was meant to be played," said Chicago head coach Mike Ditka, who practically invented the position in the early 1960s. "Playing tight end is not just catching seventy or eighty passes, but playing in the trenches and always being in the play. And that's what he does. He's the only true tight end in football. He blocks. He catches. He punishes."

At 6 feet 4 inches and 245 pounds, Bavaro is "the prototypical tight end," Giants guard Billy Ard says. "He is brutal. It takes three guys to bring him down."

Three? Three tacklers bounce off Bavaro like snowballs hitting a bus. In one of the year's most stirring plays, it took six 49ers weighing 1,265 pounds to drag him down. Ronnie Lott rode him 14 yards. "That play totally ignited us," Bill Parcells said. The Giants, trailing San Francisco 17-0 at the time, won 21-17.

"Mark has always had a blocker's mentality," said his father Anthony, a former player himself. "Unlike a lot of football players, he likes the contact. I mean, he *likes* it."

Bavaro wasn't expected to play much as a rookie with the Giants in 1985. Second-year tight end Zeke Mowatt had tied with Bobby Johnson to lead New York receivers with 48 catches in 1984. But after Mowatt's preseason knee injury in 1985, Bavaro started and came within 11 of Mowatt's 48 catches. He caught 12 against Cincinnati to set a team record.

All that was gravy to go with Bavaro's meat-and-potatoes blocking, which anchored the sweeps for Joe Morris's team-record rushing.

Bavaro went from all-rookie to all-pro with 66 catches for 1,001 yards, becoming the sixth NFL tight end ever to surpass 1,000 yards.

No wonder he was nicknamed "Rambo," although his teammates dropped the tag when Bavaro asked them to. Who wouldn't? "It's disrespectful to Vietnam veterans," Bavaro said. "Rambo exploited the Vietnam veterans. I have a lot of respect for the men who went there. A lot of my family went there."

For his resemblance to Sylvester Stallone, "Rocky" would have been a better nickname anyway. Bavaro is easy to picture running up miles of steps, even without background music. "If there's a little weakness we point out to him, the next day he's out working on it," offensive coordinator Ron Erhardt said.

He always was a dominant athlete growing up in Danvers, Massachusetts, 27 miles north of Boston. Playing both ways, he had five sacks in a high school game. Most big schools recruited him. He might have gone far in track, too, but he quit the high jump after clearing 6-6 as a junior at Notre Dame. "I weighed so much, it hurt when I landed," he says.

Bavaro isn't always a laugh a minute. He isn't always a sentence a minute. Quarterback Phil Simms said he was thrilled the time Bavaro said, "You all right?" after he'd been knocked down. Simms said it was the most Bavaro ever talked to him. "I thought, hey, the guy must really like me."

BRAD BENSON
Tackle

They even wanted to know about Brad Benson's nose. Imagine that. People don't usually notice offensive linemen themselves, let alone the bandages on their noses. But then, a lineman doesn't often pull the stage out from under the league's sack leader in one of the biggest games of the year.

It was another day at the office to Benson, just as the blood-crusted knot on his nose every week was just another annoyance. Left tackles have to block pass rushers, and they have to block out pain. They do it every week. Benson couldn't understand all the fuss just because he limited Washington's Dexter Manley to three tackles and no sacks.

"I'm supposed to block tough guys like Manley," he said. "I don't think I went out and dominated. I gave Phil time to pass. That's all I wanted to do."

Actually, quarterback Phil Simms had time to rake the yard when the Giants and Redskins, both 11-2, played for the NFC East title. Simms threw for 265 yards and 3 touchdowns. The Giants won 24-14.

The week was unusual for Benson. He doesn't often hear his teammates sing the name of the guy he'll be blocking. "Dexter, Dexter," they serenaded when the papers ran a story on Manley.

"All I heard about was Dexter," Benson said. "I probably had three ulcers waiting to play him. And I got even more nervous when I walked into the stadium and saw all those pictures of him hanging on the walls. He's more popular in Washington than the quarterback."

Benson watched film of Manley every night that week. "That's all I thought about," he said. His wife, Lisa, finally gave up and left for her mother's house on Thursday. "The problem was, I didn't know she was gone," Benson said.

Offensive linemen like to torment themselves like that. They do it to each other, too. It's usually the only way they can be absolutely sure they're more than stage scenery. The week after the game against Manley, when Benson became the first lineman to be named offensive player of the week, the other guys honored him by wearing bandages over their noses. The next week, when Benson was selected to his first NFC Pro Bowl team, they all wore his jersey number 60 to practice.

But Benson can frown with the best of them. He stews about everyone he'll have to block. "My wife says I can't enjoy myself unless I'm worrying," he says. "I'm one of those people who can't take it easy. I have to go full-speed all the time."

Benson wouldn't have lasted nine seasons otherwise. Most of the time, he's been the kind of guy coaches always are trying to replace. He's too short for a tackle, only 6 feet 3 inches. He was too small until

strength and conditioning coach Johnny Parker helped him beef up from 258 to 270. In 1984, the Giants drafted William Roberts in the first round. Roberts was 6-5 and 280, and was going to be their left tackle. Roberts missed the 1985 season with an injury, but 1986 was the year he was going to beat Benson out. It was common knowledge.

"I don't hear those things anymore," Benson said. "And when I see those stories in the newspapers, I make believe they're about somebody else." They must have been. Benson finished the season with 76 consecutive starts, going back to 1981.

Benson was the New England Patriots' seventh-round draft pick in 1977 out of Penn State. They let him go on the last cut, but he stuck around in a budget motel. He got veteran tackle Tom Neville to tutor him after practices for a while before going back home to Altoona, Pennsylvania. He kept telling himself he was as good as the big-timers he'd seen in the Hula Bowl. He just needed a chance. The call came November 15. He was substitute teaching for $15 a day, and the principal burst into his sixth-grade math class to say the Giants were on the phone. The kids cheered.

"I don't have much athletic ability," Benson says. "But you can have athletic ability and not want to do it. Thank goodness they have an offensive line in football, because if they didn't, then those of us who aren't great athletes wouldn't have a chance to play. What's good about my position is if you have a little bit of ability and you work hard, there's a chance for you."

It's not glamorous. Linemen generally are anonymous, and they figure it's just as well because fans point at them more often than they clap for them. "An offensive tackle can play a great game for sixty plays," head coach Bill Parcells says, "but if he makes a wrong move on the sixty-first play, he can wind up being crucified."

Benson compares left tackle to cornerback. "You have to run backwards, fight not to give up your lane or position and keep a guy in front of you at all times," he says. Corners can give up a touchdown on any play. Left tackles can give up the quarterback.

Cornerbacks don't often have their faces sliced, either. Benson's helmet opened the gash on his nose in the seventh game, and it reopened every week after that. The scar tissue piled up in an ugly knot, and Benson's nose began to look like a jelly roll that had been stepped on. He got it fixed in the offseason, but he was afraid his baby son Tyler wouldn't recognize him.

The fans may not, either, but they'll remember his name. As general manager George Young said, "He's a no-name guy who plays big against big-name guys."

JIM BURT
N o s e   T a c k l e

The kid didn't like being there in the first place. He thought he should have been drafted. Hadn't he forced five fumbles in one game that year for Miami? What did they want? Now he was reduced to interviewing as a free agent.

Giants general manager George Young patiently explained why he hadn't been drafted. "I told him one of the reasons was his height," Young recalled, "and I damned near had to fight him to keep him in my office. He wanted to storm out and find another team that wouldn't call him too short."

In the next six years, Jim Burt was willing to fight anyone who would keep him off the team or out of the lineup or in a hospital. He even cleaned Bill Parcells's clock when Parcells was defensive coordinator. Burt was the kind of competitor who'd throw elbows in a college pillow fight, said former Miami teammate Jim Cooper, now a Denver guard.

But after the 1986 season, the 6-foot, 260-pound nose tackle could puff out his chest and bleat, "Look at me. A dirt-bag free agent, and now I'm in the Pro Bowl."

Parcells still calls him "a pain in the butt." He says it fondly. He also says, "He's one guy I'd want in my foxhole."

"I think not getting drafted was something good," Burt says. "It made me more determined than ever. I think my hard work has kept me around here. As things get worse, I get more determined."

Too short, huh? He'd show them. All through his first training camp, Burt wore construction boots with elevated heels.

Let them just try to cut him.

They'd have to find him first. He'd hide under his bed.

"Honest, he did that," Parcells said. He also set his alarm for 6 A.M. so he could be driving around when administrative aide Vinnie Swerc was giving the bad news to players who were cut.

"They might get me at breakfast, but a *coach* was going to have to cut me himself," Burt said.

He made the team by crashing into people on kicking plays. He didn't play much on defense, but Parcells said he'd get a chance in his second game. It was close to 90 degrees, and the Giants would have to rotate nose tackles. Well, the game droned on for upwards of three plays, and Burt was pacing the sideline, getting steamed.

"I don't know what got into me," he said later. "I just went up and hit him with a forearm in the back." Parcells went flying onto the field. His headset fell off. The other players were horrified. This was a rookie, remember. "As soon as he turned around," Burt said, "I

thought, oh, no! What did I do? He said, 'Get him the [deleted] out of here,' and I thought, that's it. I'm going to be cut."

"This is not a game for well-adjusted people," Parcells says.

Burt survived the 1981 season, but Parcells promised to bring in five nose tackles the next year to take his job.

"Sure enough, at minicamp the next spring there were seven nose guards, all 270 pounds, nice and squat," Burt says. "He made my offseason miserable."

Parcells got the result he wanted. Burt beat them all. He became the starter when Bill Neill hurt his knee in the opening game of 1982. But he played only four games that year and seven the next because of a herniated disc. An enzyme injection ultimately gave him two pain-free seasons, but his back acted up again late in 1986. Burt played Super Bowl XXI facing offseason surgery and the possibility he'd never play again.

In each of his full seasons, Burt led Giants linemen in tackles. He had 10½ sacks, plus two in the 1985 playoff victory over the 49ers. Burt seized every edge he could get, down to having his jersey custom-made with a tight torso no lineman could grab onto.

Parcells kept riding Burt, "using me like a tool to get to the team," he says. When he did it all week before a 1984 game against Washington, Burt was the first to give the coach a sideline shower. It was ice water then, and it wasn't the jolly prank Harry Carson's Gatorade trick would become. Burt was furious.

"I have never met a guy that tough," Parcells says. "You could drop him from a building, from an airplane, anything. And he'd show up to play."

When Burt roamed the locker room one day, looking to borrow a razor, one of the Giants said, "Razor? I thought he just pulls out his whiskers."

His emotions never leave the surface. He cries when the Giants lose, slaps palms even with reporters when they win, and dances with the crowd when they win championships. "I still don't know how I got over that wall," Burt said of his celebration in the stands after the NFC Championship Game victory over the Redskins last January.

It's the makeup that made him Parcells's target when he had to jump on someone with a hug after the close victory against the Raiders in 1986. It's the makeup of a man who plays with passion.

"He's one of my parking-lot guys," Parcells says. "The kind who would just nod their heads, pack their bags, and be early if I told them we had a game in some shopping center parking lot, for no money, at 6 A.M. some Wednesday morning. He just loves it."

HARRY CARSON
Linebacker

The enthusiasm never lagged. Maybe that was one reason Harry Carson took losing so hard. He would throw himself into football, like Charlie Brown running up to kick the ball, but he kept landing flat on his back.

Something was missing. Late in the season, he'd catch himself at practice counting the days until he could go home for Christmas. That couldn't be right. "Let me tell you, there isn't much fun in that," Carson says.

He could have quit. He *did* quit twice. The first time, in 1980, he packed his bags in the locker room after a 35-3 Monday night loss, but head coach Ray Perkins talked him out of it. Three years later, he made it past the door. He walked out of the Giants' training camp.

But he couldn't stay away. "I really didn't want to leave the game," Carson said later. "I enjoy the game. Every time I'm on the field, I understand it could be the last time."

That's the way he plays, with a gleam in his eye and a scream in his throat. "He's still playing like a rookie," says George Martin, who has been Carson's teammate for all 11 of his NFL seasons. Carson knows he's put one over on the world. Beneath the commanding voice and the confident bearing, Carson is a real-life Peter Pan, taking money to play games. "You're still like a little kid," coach Bill Parcells once told him. "But don't change."

Carson's first five seasons were mostly bad times. He was a perennial all-pro, but the Giants went 24-52. They never were better than 6-10. That fifth year, 1980, was the worst. Carson was injured twice and missed the NFC Pro Bowl team for the only time since 1977.

He thought about joining the Air Force, to be with a winning team for a change. He told friends he wished he could have been on the rescue mission for the hostages in Iran. If he'd died, at least it would have been for something worthwhile. Now he was busting his tail for a team that couldn't win and fans that didn't understand. At Giants Stadium, he parked his car on the opposite side of the players' entrance. "I didn't want people to recognize me as a player," he said. He saw a psychologist to deal with his embarrassment at being a Giant.

In his first few years, Carson had felt sorry for players who were traded. They'd been kicked out of the club. But then he realized something. A few of those players wound up in Super Bowls with other teams. "I stopped feeling sorry for them," he said.

After the 1983 season, he started asking to be traded. The Giants wouldn't do it. They needed all the good players they had.

All he could do was leave the 1984 training camp. Parcells was furious. He said Carson didn't know the meaning of the word leadership. He said he should stop by a library and look it up. "That was pretty smart of him," Carson says. "He knew I would read that. He knew how I'd react." Carson came back—and became defensive captain.

He was a leader. He had never been anything else. He was senior class president in high school, president of the student union at South Carolina State. "It's just something I take upon myself," Carson says. "I'm very independent. Very self-sufficient. Always have been."

Carson was only 6 when his mother left home. She had no choice. His father had been laid off at the railroad, and there was no work in Florence, South Carolina. Carson's mother left his sisters in charge, found work in Newark, and sent money home. "She wanted me not to depend on other people," Carson says. "Possibly, that's one reason I'm still single."

It's a reason Parcells depends on Carson. "I don't think a day goes by when I don't talk to him about something," Parcells says. "I burden him with a lot of things. In all honesty, I probably shouldn't. Sometimes I ask him to fix things he doesn't even know are broken. But I do it anyway because he can take it. He's an amazing guy."

On the field, he calls defensive signals. He makes adjustments. He does so many intangibles, people forget he makes the plays, too.

Carson has led the Giants in tackles five times, including 185 in 1979. For comparison, their 1986 leader had 120. In one game in 1982, Carson had 25 tackles against Green Bay. He has gone to eight AFC-NFC Pro Bowls.

"You don't accomplish what he has without being someone special," Parcells says. Cleveland Browns head coach Marty Schottenheimer saw it right away. He was on the Giants' defensive staff when they drafted Carson in 1976, a 238-pound defensive end pegged for middle linebacker. "He was the best athlete that size I had ever seen," Schottenheimer says.

Now, finally, Carson is becoming well-known outside NFL videotape rooms. But for what? For dumping Gatorade on his boss. "I've been to eight Pro Bowls, and it took Gatorade to make me famous," Carson says. It's as if Laurence Olivier won an Oscar for throwing cream pies. But for Carson, his role as dumper of the barrel is the ultimate convergence of statesman and class cut-up. What good is being the best if it can't be fun?

"The only thing bad about this season," Carson said before the NFC Championship Game, "is that it eventually will have to end. If it were up to me, I would want to play until May 1. I would love that. Even after seventeen games, my body feels like I'm twenty-five again instead of thirty-three."

LEONARD MARSHALL
GEORGE MARTIN
D e f e n s i v e   E n d s

George Martin didn't want to forget the bad times. He wanted to rise above them. He wanted to look back and laugh at them, the way a successful doctor might lean back on his boat, sipping champagne, and reminiscing about that awful apartment from his medical school days, the one with running cockroaches on the floor and standing water in the sink.

He also wanted to remember how close the bad old days always were, how easy it was to fall back into them. He wanted all the Giants to know that. "I attempt to have a conversation every day with at least one of my teammates about the past," Martin said. They were like old prison-camp stories. In Martin's first nine seasons, the Giants had four coaches and a 45-85-1 record. "We were the laughing stock of the National Football League," he said.

"I tell them what it's like to be so low you have to look up to see the bottom, that fans are burning tickets and you're embarrassed to wear a Giants emblem anywhere. You're trying to get through the season so you can go home and watch the playoffs on TV. That's really a bad situation.

"I tell them sometimes how grateful they should be that it's all turned around. And I want them to know that success is a fleeting thing, and you've got to grab it while you can."

Through slim and thin, Martin helped hold the team together. He became its player representative, its chapel leader, its drug-abuse consultant. With his wife, Diane, and four children, he became the regular host for the team's Thanksgiving dinner. He organized an innovative degree-completion program for players at Fairleigh Dickinson University. "He can inspire greatness in other people just by his behavior," coach Bill Parcells said. "He's terrific. I hope he plays five more years."

One of the players Martin inspired was Leonard Marshall, the Giants second-round choice from LSU in 1983. The Giants were so excited about Marshall, they traded Gary Jeter to the Rams so Marshall could play defensive end right away. But then he lumbered into training camp at 305 pounds. "We're going to have to weigh him at the truck station on the turnpike," Bill Parcells said. Marshall's teammates said when he went to McDonald's, you could stand outside and watch the sign change to the next billion served. A club executive said, "We put Leonard on the Cambridge Diet and he ate half of Cambridge."

"When I was having rookie problems," Marshall said, "George Martin became like a big brother to me. He got me straightened out."

The coaches had cut Marshall down to help him climb. He understood that later. "I came into camp as a rookie thinking no one was tougher than I was," he said. "I figured I was going to come in and kick some tails."

Marshall changed his reckoning, not to mention his weight. He started eating broiled chicken and fish, "laying off the greasy stuff." His body fat fell from 17.5 to 14.8 percent. At 6 feet 3 inches, he became a solid 282 pounds. "He was one of the hardest-working guys we had," strength and conditioning coach Johnny Parker said.

The 1984 wild card playoff victory over the Rams put him over the hump. Marshall made four solo tackles in the Rams' backfield. "His confidence went sky-high," Parcells said.

The next season, Marshall led the NFL in sacks much of the year and wound up with 15½, a team record. He went to the AFC-NFC Pro Bowl. The league's players voted him NFL defensive lineman of the year.

"Pass rushing was like calculus to me when I first got here," Marshall said. "It was a phase of the game I had to learn. In 1985, I feel like I got my degree." In 1986, aiming for his master's, Marshall was frustrated at the new double-team attention he drew. He started slowly before finishing with 12 sacks. But after tackle Brad Benson shut out Washington's Dexter Manley, Benson said, "After going against Lenny in practice, Manley was easy."

The coaches had plucked the right string when they went after Marshall's pride. He hangs a quote in his locker from Martin Luther King. It says, "If a man is called to be a street sweeper, he should sweep streets even as Michaelangelo painted. He should sweep streets so well that all the hosts of heaven and earth will pause and say, 'Here lived a great street sweeper who did his job well.' " It still rankles him that the linebackers get the royal treatment on the defense, as if the linemen merely lace the pads for them.

"They say George needs Geritol to keep going," Marshall said. "They tell me Jim [Burt] had to hide under his bed once to keep from getting cut. And they said I was a fat defensive tackle that shouldn't have been drafted. It's almost like we got our front three off a dump truck."

Martin was hardly a savior when he joined the Giants. At his first minicamp in 1975, the eleventh-round pick from Oregon showed up with a dislocated kneecap. He said head coach Bill Arnsparger "took one look at me and said, 'There's no way you're going to be a professional football player. Go home.' "

He did. He worked back into shape. On the first play of Martin's first preseason game, veteran Jack Gregory suffered a leg injury, and

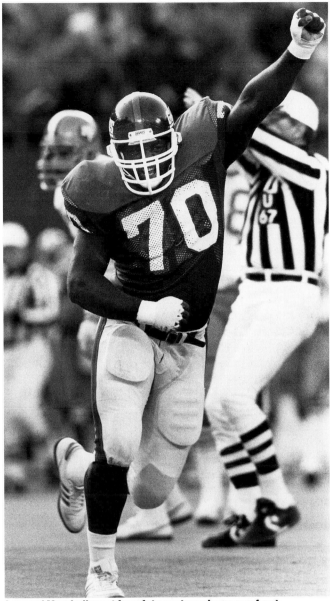

Leonard Marshall went from fat man to main man up front.

George Martin has seen it all—from the depths to the top.

Martin came in to play the rest of the game. He was a starter through 1980, when he became a pass-rush specialist. He did that for five years. Then came 1986.

Starting left end Curtis McGriff was injured in camp. Eric Dorsey, the first-round pick, wasn't ready to play. At 255 pounds, Martin would have to play nearly every down. Some blockers outweighed him by nearly 50 pounds. "He's amazing," Dorsey said. "He's as fresh in the fourth quarter as he is in the first."

Martin's starting job was no lifetime achievement award. He had played his best game in 1985, after the coaches begged him not to retire. At St. Louis, he had three sacks, recovered a fumble, and broke Bob Lilly's NFL record with his fifth touchdown as a defensive lineman, a 56-yard interception return. He made it six against Denver in 1986 with his third touchdown on an interception. He also has scored two touchdowns on fumble recoveries, one after a blocked field-goal attempt, and a seventh on offense, as a goal-line tight end. "I'm a frustrated tight end," Martin said. "I make no bones about it." He play-

ed tight end in college, until teammate Russ Francis forced him over to defense.

"I've scored more points in the NFL than I did as a college basketball player," Martin said, even before his safety in the Super Bowl. A 6-foot 4-inch backup center at Oregon, Martin always has been one of the Giants' best athletes. One day when Lawrence Taylor couldn't meet Phil Simms's challenge to throw a ball into the upper deck of Giants Stadium, Martin did it on his first try.

Martin finished his twelfth season with 86½ career sacks. In the history of the team, only six Giants have had longer careers. As Dorsey said, "He *is* the Giants." Martin embodied the perseverance of the franchise, from struggle to triumph.

"It's so unbelievable to realize the entire scope of it," he said. "I keep thinking I'm going to wake up and we'll be 3-12-1. All these years we always heard how we were heirs to a dynasty. There were years when people thought we were the pits, and rightfully so. Hopefully now the torch has been passed."

JOE MORRIS
R u n n i n g   B a c k

Joe Morris keeps a list, and it isn't short. He remembers the times people said he wasn't tall enough to be an NFL running back. He remembers when they said he couldn't block or catch or run on real grass. He remembers the 2½ years he spent holding down the Giants' bench before they let him hold up their offense. "I remember everything," he says.

When you're 5 feet 7 inches in a professional football world where 6-7 is more common, life is a series of proving points. You hardly ever hear people described as "big and scrappy."

"If you're small," Morris said, "you have to work harder than big people. That fact will always be there."

It was there the moment the Giants drafted him in the second round in 1982. They already had picked Michigan's Butch Woolfolk, a standard-sized halfback, in the first round. While Woolfolk was permitted to stumble endlessly after his pro potential, Morris said, "I had almost three years of anguish." And waiting.

It was there at Syracuse, where the athletic department couldn't bring itself to admit to a halfback so short. The Orangemen listed Morris as 5-9. They didn't own up to his true height until he had proved it moot. He broke most of the rushing records at the school that had dressed Jim Brown, Ernie Davis, Floyd Little, and Larry Csonka.

It was there, too, when he was growing up in Southern Pines, North Carolina. The neighborhood was tough. "We had rock fights like you wouldn't believe," Morris said. He made it a point to send a bigger kid home crying. "The bigger the better," he added.

Morris has been toppling big targets ever since. In the Giants' first 61 years, no one ran for more touchdowns in a career than Alex Webster, who did it 39 times in 10 seasons. Morris had 35 rushing touchdowns in his first two full seasons. He had 21 in 1985; he added 14 in 1986 to boost his career total to 40. He finished the 1986 season with 16 100-yard games, five three-touchdown games, and two consecutive 1,000-yard seasons. They all were team records. After 1,516 yards in 1986, Morris's career rushing total of 3,555 was only 1,083 yards behind Webster's mark.

Morris isn't small. He's just short. He weighs 195 pounds. "If he were 6-2, he'd weigh 240," general manager George Young says. He breaks tackles with upper legs so explosive, Bears defenders compare him to Walter Payton, the all-time rushing leader.

"He's a strange combination," said Denver linebacker Karl Mecklenburg. "He's a small power runner."

"Defensive players see a runner 5-foot-7," Morris said, "and they expect to encounter 160 pounds. I weigh thirty-five pounds more than

that. I'm not a scatback guy. I'm a 6-2 guy in a 5-7 body. The only time I notice my size is when I watch game films. I notice how big those other guys are compared to me."

Strength and conditioning coach Johnny Parker has to keep explaining himself when he calls Morris one of the Giants' strongest players. "Not pound-for-pound—just one of the strongest," he says. Morris can squat and stand up three times with 555 pounds on his shoulders, nearly triple his weight.

"This guy hits the hole faster than anyone I've been around in twenty years," offensive line coach Fred Hoaglin said. With that acceleration, he can wait until the last instant before committing himself. He can be more sure of picking a good hole. Offensive coordinator Ron Erhardt said patience is Morris's greatest attribute.

Morris's first start came with more patience than he'd bargained for. It was the Giants' ninth game in 1984, his third season. Morris ran for three touchdowns in a 37-13 victory over Washington, the two-time NFC champion.

In the wild-card playoff victory that year, Morris ran 61 yards for a touchdown, alternately trampling and scampering through the Los Angeles Rams' defense. A penalty canceled the play, but not before it "gave him the confidence that he could, in fact, break tackles," George Young said. Since then, Morris has been, in Young's words, "our home-run runner."

The short jokes started rolling off his back like hapless tacklers. Morris even got a big kick out of former Giants punter Dave Jennings's gag, when he held his hand waist high and said, "This is a high five for Joe Morris." He hears them all every year.

"I just say, 'Ha-ha...pretty funny,' " Morris said. "Then I put on my helmet."

Morris learned to climb the highest obstacles from his father, an army sergeant who would dump all his son's bedroom drawers and make him clean the room all over if one thing were out of place. "What Dad instilled in me was the knowledge that I could do things right if I just wanted to work hard enough," Morris said. What Master Sgt. Morris raised was a competitor who once refused to leave a game with a concussion until somebody hid his helmet.

"I've always got to prove myself," Morris said. "It's a never-ending battle. I just want people to say that Joe Morris does his job, not that he's too small. Maybe one day, when I'm fifty years old and I'm on a street corner, they're going to say, 'You know, that little guy was a pretty good player.' "

Maybe they're even starting to say it now.

PHIL SIMMS
Quarterback

The critics got a running start. Phil Simms hadn't even come to New York when Giants fans started booing him. They booed his name at the draft.

"Even the people back home were shocked when I was drafted in the first round," Simms said. "The next day, the Louisville papers were critical of the Giants. They as much as said I had no right being drafted that high." Okay, so Morehead State wasn't exactly Football U. Neither was Louisiana Tech, and Terry Bradshaw did all right. The scouts had been drooling over Simms all through his senior year. Giants fans are among the most knowledgeable in sports. They'd seen his name projected as a first-round possibility.

But there was something about Simms that made fans climb walls. Even in 1984, when he finally played a full season, they didn't let up. Simms was one of three players to pass for 4,000 yards that year. Dan Marino and Neil Lomax couldn't have bought their own drinks in Miami and St. Louis without wearing masks. Simms? All anyone said about him was he threw too many interceptions.

The interceptions always have been a sore point. They're not good. But Joe Namath threw a lot of interceptions, too. It's the price of being aggressive. On the charisma scale, that should work in Simms's favor, not get him showered with eggs, golf balls, and oranges during pregame introductions.

But Simms doesn't have that swagger of an aggressive quarterback, that defiant sneer. He's a nice guy. Fans don't like him because he's too likable. He acts more like a neighbor than a leader.

Simms once joked that if they made a TV series about him, they could call it "Life in the Slow Lane." Giants linemen have made him an honorary Suburbanite, which doesn't quite have the menacing ring of an honorary Hog or an honorary Black and Blues Brother. Simms isn't the only NFL quarterback to hang out with his linemen. Jim McMahon does it, too. But there's a difference. McMahon drinks beer with linemen, Simms lifts weights with them. When a Giant mentions this, he does it with an adoring gleam.

But, Simms leads. He's a rock his teammates can lean on. "There was a time when I felt the offense didn't have a leader," Lawrence Taylor said. "They were just a bunch of guys out there trying not to lose a game. They didn't have one person to really tie them all together, to lead them. Phil has really taken that responsibility. He's done a real good job."

Simms wouldn't have inspired that confidence by throwing helmets when things went wrong. Simms never bad-mouthed his receivers or linemen, and they appreciated it. He didn't even grit his teeth at adversity. That would have just wasted energy. Simms poured all he had into simply getting better. "He willed himself into being an outstanding performer," general manager George Young said.

"That's one tough guy," said Jim Burt, the nose tackle who embodies toughness. "To go through what he's gone through. And the way he's kept his confidence."

For five seasons, however, Simms went through a roller-coaster ride that was mostly downhill. He got off on the right foot. He won five of his first six starts after the Giants were 0-5 in 1979. But they finished 6-10. Then shoulder separations knocked him out of the last three games in 1980 and the last five in 1981. He missed all of 1982 with a knee injury. By 1983, when Bill Parcells became coach, Scott Brunner had been filling in for Simms so long, Parcells didn't want to make a change. But when Brunner got hurt Simms had his chance. He threw 13 passes before he caught his thumb on a piece of tape that hung from the wrist of the Eagles' Dennis Harrison. The freak play resulted in a compound fracture, and Simms was out for the year.

"I was probably lucky not to get the job that year," Simms said. "Scott played himself off the team. I might have done the same thing." No quarterback could have turned back that 3-12-1 tidal wave. Simms called his benching "the turning point" of his career. He wasn't crazy about it then. The injuries and the losing had given him enough self-doubts. Now someone was saying he wasn't good enough.

"Confidence is a funny thing," Simms says. "You can go around saying you have it, but you really don't until you have some success. There were times I thought I'd never have the chance to show what I thought I could do. There were other times I began to wonder if I was really as good as I thought I was, that I might not have what it takes to play in this league."

Simms didn't flinch, though. He always has stood as tall in the face of critics and pass rushers. Chicago head coach Mike Ditka said, "He holds the ball to the last second as well as anybody." Just as he's done with his career, Simms waits with determined patience as long as he can to give a play a chance. "I've seen him take some unbelievable hits," tackle Brad Benson says. He has found out about many touchdown passes while he was flat on his back.

The confidence started resurfacing after the 1985 season. It was his first AFC-NFC Pro Bowl. McMahon was top dog, but Simms's three touchdown passes brought the NFC back to win. "One of the most exciting things I'd done," he said. The feat won him the game's most-valuable-player trophy.

Still, when the 1986 Giants passed the halfway mark in first place, it generally was believed they'd gotten there in spite of Simms. The defense and Joe Morris carried them to 5-1 in games 5 through 10. Injuries depleted the wide receivers, and Simms grew cautious. Parcells pulled him aside. "I told Phil, 'I think you're a great quarterback,'" he said. "'It doesn't matter what anyone thinks of you except me and your teammates. You got to be what you are by being daring and fearless. So let's go. Be yourself.'"

Simms made big plays in each of the next four victories. Fourth-and-17 late against Minnesota. Third-and-21 late against Denver. Three touchdowns in nine minutes after San Francisco led 17-0 at halftime. Two touchdowns on third-and-long against Washington, and another third-and-long play that set up a touchdown. He was a 62.4-percent passer in those four games, throwing for six touchdowns and averaging 278 yards a game.

"I won some games the way people think a quarterback should," Simms said.

He didn't win all the fans over, but he had himself in his corner again. "The better he gets, the harder he works," Parcells said.

"Sometimes you get into a groove," Simms said, "and whether it's hitting a tennis ball or golfing or shooting baskets, things start going well." Simms got into that groove for the best Super Bowl performance any quarterback ever had. He was 22-for-25 passing, clearly the most valuable player. He also had his fourth consecutive playoff game without an interception.

"The thing that's most impressive about Phil Simms," Denver head coach Dan Reeves said, "is when they put the pressure on him to do something, he comes through for them."

"For our team, Simms is absolutely the best guy," Parcells says. That's starting to dawn on his critics, too. Even before the Super Bowl, Young told of an articulate fan who had written regularly to demand Young find a new quarterback. After the NFC Championship Game victory over Washington, the fellow wrote, "Perhaps. . .just perhaps. . .Phil Simms is the quarterback for this club."

LAWRENCE TAYLOR
L i n e b a c k e r

They've tried tackles, guards, backs, and tight ends. They've tried double-teams and triple-teams. They've tried everything. They've had little success. When Lawrence Taylor charges, the NFL listens. For the loud thud.

Taylor is remarkably tough, relentlessly reckless, and fiercely driven. His typical sideline exhortation is, "Let's go out there like a bunch of crazed dogs and have some fun!" He flings his body around like a stunt man. "He has a motor that never goes off," said Washington assistant head coach-offense Joe Bugel.

"I love to hit and get hit," Taylor said. "When you're yelling and your eyes turn red and you feel like slapping your mother, that's when you know you're ready to play ball."

But there's even more than that. It took more than a wild streak for Taylor to redefine a position. Sure, there were other blitzing weakside linebackers in a 3-4 defense before 1981, when Taylor burst into the NFL. But Taylor set the specs for the job.

For six years, coaches have been begging scouts to find them "another Lawrence Taylor," as if it's some brand name that comes off the rack. He's not. He's an original.

He stands 6 feet 3 inches, weighs 243, and runs like a halfback.

"The best defensive player I have ever seen," says Sam Huff, the Pro Football Hall of Fame linebacker. Huff also calls him, "the fastest linebacker I've ever seen." Taylor can rush the passer, then turn around after the ball is thrown and catch the receiver downfield. On the next play, he can toss a 270-pound guard aside as if the guy were a sawhorse.

Taylor inspired Washington head coach Joe Gibbs to use the one-back offense that has wound up in most teams' playbooks. "Putting another tight end on the line of scrimmage was the only way to block Lawrence Taylor," Gibbs said. Not that it's foolproof security.

"He affects every play, no matter what side of the field you're going to," Cincinnati offensive coordinator Bruce Coslet said. "We changed our blocking schemes because of him."

Taylor calls it an honor when teams do that. It affirms his place in the evolutionary cycle, somewhere between man and Superman. He doesn't follow most players' standards. He *is* the standard.

Most players can't make three sacks in a game with one arm useless from injury. Taylor not only did it on Monday night against Washington, he played golf the next day.

Most players need to lift weights to stay healthy and strong. Taylor visits the weight room mainly out of curiosity. One day he saw players jumping flat-footed from the ground to elevated boxes, a drill for leg explosiveness. The highest box was 42 inches. "He jumped up on the forty-two-inch box with no more effort than you'd make jumping up to the curb," strength and conditioning coach Johnny Parker said.

"Lawrence has a Superman image," Parker said. "Superman didn't lift weights. He's almost compelled to uphold the image."

It's a heavy burden, even just on the field. John Madden compares him to a baseball player who hits .400 early in his career. "So then he never gets another good pitch to hit," Madden said. "Now, they always have a big guy on Lawrence blocking him." And when Taylor doesn't get through, they wonder why.

However, in 1985, after four years as the NFL Players' Association linebacker of the year and two years as NFL defensive player of the year, Taylor was less than himself. He had 13½ sacks, a career high, and he made his fifth consecutive NFC Pro Bowl squad, but, as former Cowboys wide receiver Drew Pearson said, "It seemed like he was getting to a lot of plays about a half-step late." Never mind that it was still a half-step earlier than most players.

Something was wrong.

Taylor had leaked a clue the previous year. "Sunday is a different world," he said. "It's like a fantasy world, which I'd rather live in. Then I go back to the rest of the world and that's when the trouble starts."

That's where reckless abandon is frowned on. In college, Taylor had a hobby of trashing frat houses, as though they were end sweeps. In his six seasons with the Giants, reporters have counted at least four cars he has crashed. As general manager George Young says, "He overdoes most things, on and off the field."

After the 1985 season, his lifestyle went careening into headlines. He admitted spending time as an outpatient in Houston for rehabilitation from an addiction he would not specify.

"He said he'd get his act together, and he has," Young said. And how!

In 1986, Taylor became the third defensive player to be named league MVP (the Giants' Andy Robustelli earned that honor in 1962, and the Los Angeles Rams' Merlin Olsen in 1974). Taylor had 15 sacks in a seven-game stretch. He led the league with 20½, and that understated his impact. "He's able to rush a passer against any offensive lineman," Dallas backfield coach Al Lavan said.

Philadelphia personnel director Joe Woolley called him "the most dominating player in football—offense or defense."

Taylor still called himself "a just, plain wild dude. I don't really

care what other people expect of me, or what society says I'm supposed to do. I do it my way and try to get the job done that way. I don't try to act like high society, or go to high-society places. I hang with regular people. I make mistakes like everybody else, but I'm just doing my job."

"He still goes out and has a good time," linebacker Andy Headen said. "It's just that he saves a little more for Sunday."

At the same time, the Giants saved Taylor for what he did best. "And that is rushing the passer," defensive coordinator Bill Belichick said.

He seldom played in coverage, for the same reason Babe Ruth ultimately gave up pitching.

"When he hits you," said Jay Schroeder, the Redskins' young AFC-NFC Pro Bowl quarterback, "you have to take inventory. You have to see if everything's still hooked up. You start shaking. You make

sure your legs are there, and your arms, and everything else."

Even as a rookie in 1981, Taylor was brazen enough about pass rushing to wink at the quarterback. So what if they knew he was coming? They still had to stop him. "When Lawrence Taylor is pass rushing, it's like a cop putting sirens on top of his car," safety Beasley Reece said.

One thing was missing, though. Taylor wanted so much to be with a winner, he volunteered for kicking squads. He even offered to play tight end in 1983.

"There's nothing like hearing people say, 'Oooo, wow!' when you say you play for the Giants," he said. "I've heard just that reaction when someone mentions the Raiders or the Cowboys."

Now that Superman has a super team, they not only can't block Taylor, they can't knock him, either.

AND THE REST OF THE CAST OF 45

Game balls are football's equivalent of a bull's ears. They go to the victors, who award them to the stars. The Giants rarely give game balls. The Giants don't like to distinguish stars because in football, the chorus doesn't just back up the stars. It props them up. "One man doesn't win the game," coach Bill Parcells said. "Forty-five do."

The Giants won the Super Bowl with the best chorus in the NFL.

Take their offensive linemen. Linemen don't usually get game balls anyway. They don't have statistics. They don't have personalities, as far as most fans are concerned. They're one big 10-legged animal. The really notorious ones have nicknames.

The Giants' linemen called themselves the Suburbanites. Now *there's* a fear-inspiring nickname. You'd hate to run into those guys in a dark parking lot. But the handle fit, even if it did sound awfully white-collar.

There was nothing bureaucratic about the layers of protection the Suburbanites gave ball carriers. By the end of the season, they were doing the same for Phil Simms.

Besides, these guys *were* suburbanites.

"That's us," center Bart Oates said. "A wife, a family life, small kids, a grill in the backyard. We mow our own yards and shovel our own driveways. Yup. It fits."

It started out as Parcells's backhanded compliment. In 1985, he groused, "What you want are guys from Toledo, Detroit, places like that. Instead, we've got guys from Watchung, New Jersey, and Hollywood, Florida. That's the kind of places where your mama drives you to practice in the station wagon and makes sure your uniform's clean. But they've done the job, I guess."

Left guard Billy Ard was from Watchung, near New York City. Right guard Chris Godfrey was from Hollywood, near Miami. Left tackle Brad Benson was from Lakemont, near Altoona, Pennsylvania. Right tackle Karl Nelson was from DeKalb, Illinois, near Chicago. Oates was from Albany, Georgia, a city without the smokestacks and steel Parcells had in mind.

And now they all lived comfortably in north Jersey, with professional educations and safe lifestyles.

"I might have one beer with the boys," Godfrey said, "but I get my kicks by going home, trimming the hedges, and taking out the garbage. The name fits us off the field. But I think our line plays like a bunch of city kids, short of using knives and blackjacks. We're best when we're tenacious and on the attack." •

Godfrey was the player Benson felt bad about when his big game against Washington made him the line's official village manager and NFC Pro Bowl representative. "I looked at the stat sheet and Dave Butz had no tackles, no assists, and no sacks," Benson said. "Chris had shut him out."

Only Nelson was a high draft pick, a third-rounder. Godfrey was cut by three NFL teams as a defensive lineman before the Michigan Panthers of the USFL made him a guard. Ard was an eighth-round pick after his family, lifelong Giants fans, unfurled a banner at NFL draft headquarters. It urged the Giants to "Make Ard Your Guard." They did, along with seven other guards in training camp.

"I just busted my butt and paid attention," Ard said.

"We're not the biggest or the strongest line in the game," Nelson said, "but we work well together."

They also like each other. "They hang around together, lift weights together," Parcells said. "Maybe some people have doubts about their ability, but they're smart and they don't make mistakes."

Nelson was an academic All-America as an engineering student at Iowa State. Ard, from Wake Forest, is a stockbroker in the offseason.

Oates has an accounting degree from Brigham Young and goes to law school. Godfrey has a business degree from Michigan and works in a bank. "He's the resident philosopher," Benson said before the Super Bowl. "He probably read Dante on the flight here."

They were backed up capably by William Roberts, Brian Johnston, and Damian Johnson, the 290-pound guard who played some goal-line fullback without being asked to lend his name to half of America's marketplace.

After the 1985 season, running back Joe Morris thanked his blockers by buying them watches. "Last year, we put in a request for chain saws," Oates said.

Morris can't overlook Maurice Carthon, perhaps the league's best blocking back. When Morris got the use of a car for being Giants' player of the week, he gave Carthon the keys. "He's a truck," Parcells says. "He's a good, solid, unselfish player."

Even growing up in Osceola, Arkansas, Carthon admired good blocking. When everyone else wanted to be O. J. Simpson, Carthon wanted to be Jim Braxton, Simpson's fullback. "My brother James and I would watch games on TV," Carthon said, "and he'd say, 'Watch Braxton. Look at what he's doing.'"

Carthon got a taste for carrying the ball with the New Jersey Generals, before he spent a season blocking for Herschel Walker's 2,411-yard rushing total in 1985. During the previous year, Carthon had a

An outstanding blocker, Maurice Carthon (44) also could run behind guard Billy Ard (67) and tackle William Roberts.

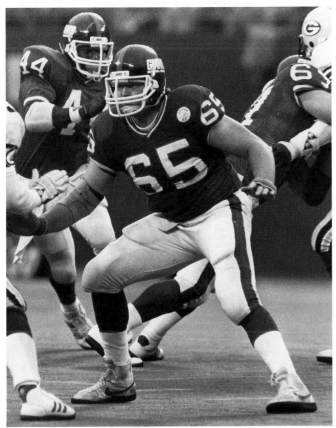

Center Bart Oates went to law school in his spare time.

Bobby Johnson led the wide receivers with 31 catches.

chance to carry the ball and ran for 1,042 yards and 11 touchdowns.

"If I don't run the ball because I'm such a good blocking back, that's one thing and I can live with it," he said. "I like blocking. It frees up the running back for that extra shot he needs to get in the clear. But when I do it, when I let him get away, I'm wishing it was me."

With fullback George Adams out for the season, it took more than Carthon and Morris to pick up the slack. As the Giants' number-one draft choice in 1985, Adams had run for 498 yards and caught 31 passes for 389. Lee Rouson, who'd missed nearly all his 1985 rookie season with a knee injury, chipped in with 179 yards on the ground and 121 on eight catches, scoring two of his three touchdowns in the season finale against Green Bay. Ottis Anderson came in a trade from St. Louis after the fifth game and happily gave up his chance to move up the all-time top-10 rushing ladder for a chance to play in the Super Bowl, where he scored the Giants' last touchdown. With 81 rushing yards for the Giants, Anderson finished the season two yards behind Larry Csonka's tenth-place total of 8,081.

Tony Galbreath finished his eleventh NFL season two yards shy of 4,000 yards, but he remained the most prolific receiving back ever with 464 catches, leading Walter Payton by five. That gave him one fewer year and 172 more catches than the Giants' five wide receivers combined.

Those receivers took a public flogging. They were blamed for not getting open when Simms took 40 sacks in the first 12 games.

They were blamed for dropping balls, including five in Simms's 8-for-18 day at Philadelphia. "They took a lot of abuse during the year, but all of them made big plays," Simms said. They improved, as they will in 1987. Bobby Johnson, Lionel Manuel, and Phil McConkey were in their third seasons, Solomon Miller was a rookie, and Stacy Robinson might as well have been after his injury in 1985.

Johnson led the team with 31 catches and became the clutch receiver on long-yardage plays against Minnesota and Denver. Manuel returned after his knee injury in the fourth game, and Simms leaned on him for big catches in the NFC Championship Game. He and Johnson had caught 82 and 81, respectively, in their first two seasons.

Robinson, the biggest and fastest of the top three, had 29 catches, despite an injury that sidelined him three weeks. "There's some talent there," Parcells said. "There's just not much experience."

"We have guys who go over the middle to catch the ball," McConkey said. "We don't have those glamor wideouts who run those pretty-boy routes down the sidelines on camera. We get our hair mussed, our helmets cracked. We don't play pretty-boy football. We play to win. We don't care how it looks."

A Cowboys coach once said, "McConkey could catch a punt in a rock slide." Kick returns were the reason the Giants traded an eleventh-round pick to get him back four weeks after cutting him. "How could I be bitter at an organization that gave me an opportunity at twenty-seven to live my dream?" he said at the Super Bowl.

McConkey went to Navy because it was the only big-time team that would take a 145-pound high school senior, and he became the first Middie since Roger Staubach to make the NFL after his five-year hitch. "The reason I pursued this dream," McConkey said, "is I didn't want to sit in front of a television set when I was forty-five or fifty and wonder, what if?"

In his ninth year, quarterback Jeff Rutledge was wondering if he could start for another team. Simms's consecutive-game streak ran to 48, tied for tops in the league at quarterback.

Zeke Mowatt had to wonder about fate, too. The 1983 free agent had led the team with 48 catches in 1984. But he missed the 1985 season with a knee injury, then worked hard and painfully back into shape only to find an all-pro— Bavaro— at his tight end spot.

Still, Mowatt scored three touchdowns in 1986, including one in the Super Bowl. He also kept blocking like a bulldozer.

There didn't seem to be anywhere for those five defensive rookies from the first two draft rounds to play, but they made themselves at home in the special-situation lineups.

First-round end Eric Dorsey's three postseason sacks tied Leonard Marshall for the team lead. He looked like the man who'll finally let 13-year-veteran George Martin give in to his age. No telling how good Martin still can be with some rest. In the Super Bowl, Dorsey spelled him on the series before Martin got his safety on Elway.

Mark Collins was the only regular rookie starter. He stepped in after Elvis Patterson's injury and made the NFL's all-rookie team. Erik Howard started two games when nose tackle Jim Burt's back gave out, and the run defense remained strong. Thomas (Pepper) Johnson, the special teams player who put pepper on his cereal as a kid, was going to be groomed to replace inside linebacker Harry Carson.

Johnson seemed to be ahead of schedule when he spelled Gary Reasons against the pass. But the underrated Reasons has been penciled out of lineups before, and he's spent two full seasons getting in the way of whoever has the ball.

With Greg Lasker, the Giants were able to use six defensive backs and still stuff the run.

By cramming a linebacker into his quick, strong safety body, Lasker "gave us flexibility we never had," defensive backs coach Len Fontes said.

The Giants used 18 regulars in their various defenses. Jerome Sally had 3½ sacks in limited action as the pass-rushing nose tackle. Andy Headen was a passing-down linebacker. Even the seventh and eighth linebackers, Byron Hunt and Robbie Jones, were better than many teams' starters. Safety Tom Flynn had an interception and a blocked punt for a touchdown playing slivers of just two games.

The Giants' secondary was better known for giving receivers alligator arms. Arms do grow short when they feel a collision coming on. Even free safety Terry Kinard, shy and quiet off the field, "reminds me of Jack Tatum," said strong safety Kenny Hill, the ex-Raider who's both a connoisseur of arm-shortening hits and a Yale graduate in molecular biophysics. At the Super Bowl, second-year safety Herb Welch said, "I'm pinching myself so much I have bruises." He started after Kinard's season-ending knee injury in the fourteenth game.

"Hill is like having a coach on the field," defensive coordinator Bill Belichick said.

Elvis Patterson may never shake the nickname Toast, from all the times he was burned as a rookie in 1984. But receivers don't shake him much anymore. He started in the playoffs, after Collins's injury. Teams went after him. They came up empty. That's fine, he said. He can take it. As Hill said at the Super Bowl, "I doubt they'll try to throw the ball deep against Perry Williams. He's one of the fastest guys in the NFL. Not many people get behind him." Only his teammates. When it comes to winning, they all get behind each other.

Safety Terry Kinard (43) and cornerback Perry Williams.

Mark Collins started as a rookie corner.

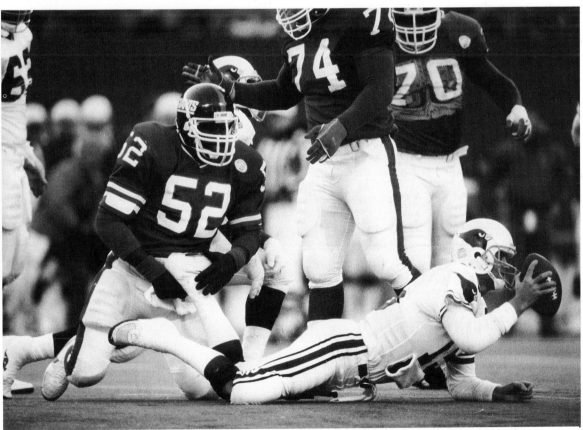

Rookie linebacker Thomas (Pepper) Johnson (52) came off the bench to make 37 tackles, including two sacks.

THE REGULAR SEASON

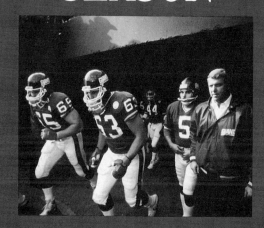

FROM SEPTEMBER 8
THROUGH DECEMBER 21

THEY'RE OFF…WHOOPS!

Cowboys 31, Giants 28

The Super Bowl Express began with the hood up and the hazard lights flashing. This was supposed to be the Giants' new, improved defense? It gave up 384 yards in the 31-28 Monday night loss at Dallas. Worse yet, the two-minute defense bent so far, it folded with a crease. The Cowboys drove for a field goal as the first half ended, then for the winning touchdown with 1:16 left in the game.

The Giants could have won it. *Should* have won it, really, just as they should have beaten the Cowboys when they lost 30-29 and 28-21 the previous year. This time, they came from 14 points down but squandered two leads in the second half. "It's obvious we have a lot of work to do," head coach Bill Parcells said. Even scarier, the Cowboys appeared to be more improved than their 1985 division champions now that they had Herschel Walker.

"He [Walker] won the game for us, no question about it," Dallas quarterback Danny White said. "He made some huge plays." Walker scored twice, including the winning touchdown, and his 23-yard run with a screen pass started the winning drive.

Walker had been a Concorde among helicopters in the players' evacuation from the dying USFL. In three seasons in the USFL, he rushed for 5,562 yards; the Cowboys rewarded that success with a rich five-year contract.

Walker wasn't expected to play much against the Giants. He'd been practicing only two weeks. But Dallas head coach Tom Landry showed right away how Walker could thrive alongside perennial all-pro Tony Dorsett. Neither had to play fullback, either. The Cowboys used a three-back offense, with Walker usually flanking out to a sideline. Walker would wait his turn as a runner.

Astonishingly, his turn came in his first NFL game. As Dorsett scored the game's first touchdown on a 36-yard screen pass, he sprained an ankle. Walker was inserted as the new tailback. The next time he got the ball, he gave Dallas a

14-0 lead with a one-yard dive, cashing in on the fumbled snap Cowboys defensive tackle Randy White had recovered at the Giants' 2.

The Giants seemed unfazed. They tied the score on Phil Simms's touchdown passes to Bobby Johnson and Stacy Robinson in the last 1:49 of the first half. The bad start was erased. Now all they had to do was play out the last 25 seconds until halftime and keep pouring it on after intermission.

Those 25 seconds went down like a fishbone. Three big gains moved Dallas 54 yards to the Giants' 18. On the last two, passes for 23 and 18 yards, wide receiver Gordon Banks caught the ball in front of the Giants' new Nickel back, rookie Mark Collins. With two seconds left, Rafael Septien came in to kick a 35-yard field goal, giving Dallas a 17-14 advantage.

Walker gave back his touchdown in the second half when he fumbled the ball to Giants linebacker Harry Carson at the Cowboys' 14. Joe Morris got the score on a 2-yard run. Dallas matched that touchdown on Thornton Chandler's 1-yard score on a pass from White early in the fourth quarter. Carson later recovered another fumble, and the Giants turned it into a 28-24 lead with 5:24 left when Johnson tipped an underthrown ball, then outleaped cornerback Ron Fellows for a 44-yard touchdown.

The Cowboys' last chance began with 2:10 to play. Within a minute, they had a third-and-5 situation at the Giants' 10. Dallas lined up in its spread formation. White started back to pass, but he gave the ball to Walker instead. The middle was free, and all Walker had to overcome on his touchdown run were a couple of arm tackles. "We were expecting a pass," linebacker Carl Banks said.

The defense wore out, Parcells said. Not every player...but some. That wasn't supposed to happen. The Giants had drafted five defenders in the first two rounds in 1986 so everyone could stay fresh. Parcells said he would begin rotating players. "Our players were disappointed and so was I," Parcells said.

Giants quarterback Phil Simms danced away from Dallas's Randy White, as he passed for 300 yards and three touchdowns. But the Cowboys ruined New York's opener with a come-from-behind 31-28 victory, their third in a row over the Giants.

DEFUSING THE CHARGERS

Giants 20, Chargers 7

All week, Bill Parcells heard advice. If he didn't come up with some brilliant plan, everyone knew San Diego quarterback Dan Fouts would toast his defense, slice it up, and serve it with jelly. Fouts had been doing that for years. The Chargers had scored 50 points the week before against Miami; they had totaled 30 or more in 28 of their last 58 games. They made scoreboards whir like electric fans in August.

"Some people said you've got to blitz Fouts and pressure him," Parcells said. "If you blitz him, they'll score fifty points against you."

Parcells had researched the subject, too. The Giants' coaches had consulted their counterparts at Denver and Kansas City. The Chargers' AFC West rivals had seen a lot of the shell game San Diego plays, in which receivers are moved before the snap. The Broncos and Chiefs helped the Giants understand what to ignore and what to watch for. "We've been studying that offense since last February," Parcells said. "The way they interchange everybody, designed to open something quickly on every play, makes you very nervous."

Blitzing robs a quarterback of time, but Fouts doesn't need much time. So the Giants would attack the Chargers' receivers, hitting them at the line and covering them gang-to-man.

"Mama said there would be days like this," Fouts said after the Giants won their home opener 20-7. All of the Chargers' six possessions in the second half ended in turnovers. With the door slammed on his quick pass plays, Fouts threw five interceptions for only the third time in 14 pro seasons, and the first time since 1980.

"It seemed wherever I wanted to throw the ball, the Giants were already there," Fouts said. "I don't think I was tipping anything off. I think they just did a lot of homework and have a great defense."

"We did a lot of soul-searching all week," said Giants nose tackle Jim Burt, recalling the defensive collapse against Dallas. "It was the toughest week of my life. We got knocked to our knees emotionally. The defense was supposed to be the backbone of this team, and we were the weak link."

As Harry Carson said, "A lot of people matured against the Chargers." Nickel back Mark Collins had his first NFL interception. Strong safety Kenny Hill had two. Free safety Terry Kinard had two interceptions (a third was nullified by a penalty) and a fumble recovery, all with a shoulder so bruised he could barely lift his arm.

The Chargers' only score came on a 43-yard drive after Lionel James's 19-yard punt return. Fouts's 29-yard pass to Gary Anderson merely cut the Giants' lead to 10-7. They already had Joe Cooper's short field goal and Joe Morris's one-yard touchdown, which Kinard had set up by recovering a fumble by James at the Chargers' 32.

The Giants had chances to score more points than they did. Two first-and-goal set-ups at the 2 yielded only Cooper's early field goal. Morris, still rusty from his training camp holdout, lost 17 yards on 8 carries, had 6 carries for no gain and 5 for just one yard.

But Morris was getting there. His other 11 carries gained 95 yards. The balance was returning to the offense. Simms threw for exactly 300 yards for the second consecutive week, but the run-pass ratio was 45-42, much better than 28-48 in the opening game at Dallas.

The Giants controlled the ball for 12:10 of the first 15 minutes and 39:44 of the entire 60. The Chargers' seven turnovers were a big reason for the Giants' dominance, but so was New York's 9-for-18 success on third down. Those weren't a bunch of quarterback sneaks, either. The Giants were 5-for-10 when they needed at least 10 yards. Simms completed third-down passes when the Chargers *knew* he would pass, and he was doing it on a day so many wide receivers limped off that the Giants' third-string quarterback, Jeff Hostetler, had to play the position.

Giants wide receiver Lionel Manuel clutched a 12-yard touchdown pass from Phil Simms, with San Diego cornerback Wayne Davis hanging on. On defense, the Giants forced seven turnovers and stifled the Chargers 20-7.

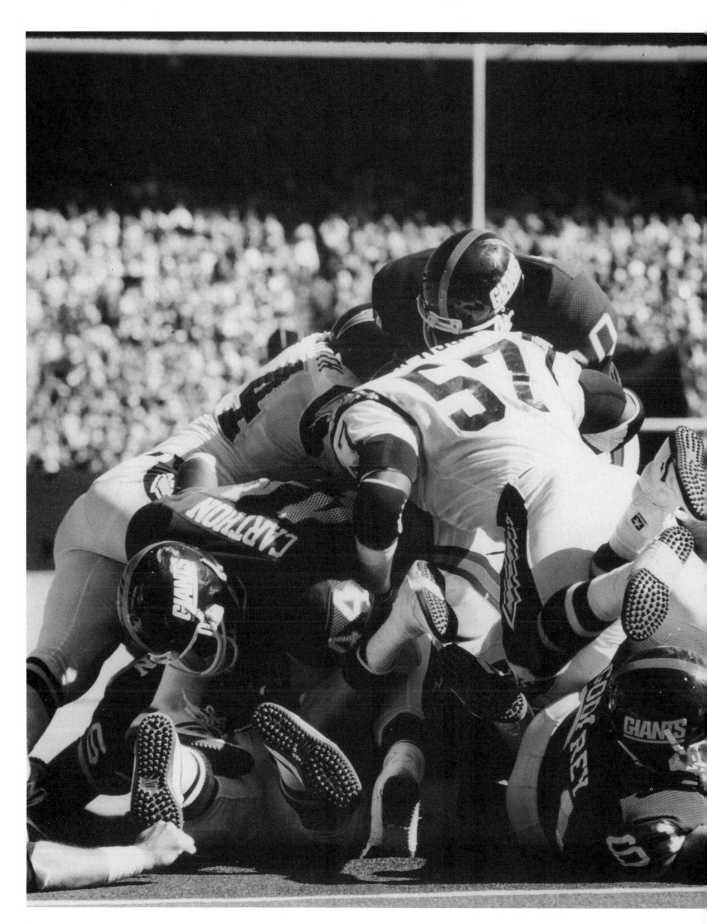

Joe Morris (left) squeezed between San Diego linebackers
Thomas Benson (57) and Billy
Ray Smith (54) to score New
York's first touchdown. After the
game, Giants head coach Bill
Parcells accepted a congratula-
tory handshake from San Diego
head coach Don Coryell.

WINNING A SLUGFEST
Giants 14, Raiders 9

Any team that prides itself on raising welts in order to raise a championship flag has to prove itself against the Raiders. It didn't matter that Los Angeles was 0-2 going into week three. If you wanted a welt-raising, head-razing, sawed-off-shotgun of a football team, the Raiders still were the model.

Two acceptable images have emerged for NFL champions. There are the Silicon Valley wizards, with the computerized offenses of teams such as San Francisco and Miami. And there are the Back Alley scourges, the street fighters from places like Los Angeles and Chicago, who take no prisoners.

The Giants already had their blue-collar aura when they went to Los Angeles. By beating the Raiders 14-9, they graduated from grimy fingernails to bloody knuckles, from card-carrying pipefitters to crowd-scaring pipe wielders. After the victory, the Giants' first ever against the Raiders in four tries, Raiders head coach Tom Flores confirmed the Giants' status. "I don't remember a defense playing us that physical," Flores said. "We had trouble making our reliable plays work, the ones that always do. I've got to feel that's the best defense we'll face all season."

The Giants not only beat the Raiders, they beat them up. They not only broke Marcus Allen's NFL-record streak of 11 consecutive 100-yard games, they sent him limping from the game early in the second half with a sprained ankle and bruised ribs. Allen finished with just 40 yards on 15 carries and never returned to form in 1986.

Quarterback Jim Plunkett felt the Giants' presence, too. In his first start in nearly a year, the 16-year veteran was hit, hurried, and humbled. Safety Terry Kinard and linebacker Andy Headen knocked the ball loose from him on sacks that ended scoring threats at the Giants' 12- and 26-yard lines.

There's more to beating the Raiders than giving punishment. The Giants took it, too. Phil Simms shook off a three-sack first half to go 10 for 12 for 139 yards and two touchdowns in the second half.

Tight end Mark Bavaro recalled old Raiders workhorse Dave Casper as he lugged tacklers like backpacks. His six catches for 106 yards included a 29-yard gain in which he carried safety Stacey Toran 12 yards.

Joe Morris hung in, too. After seven first-half carries for 17 yards, he finished with 18 for 110, the first 100-yard rusher against the Raiders in 19 regular-season games. Given the closeness of the score, his 52-yard burst in the fourth quarter probably was the Giants' first big play of the season.

There wasn't much for the scrapbook in the first half. The Raiders scored twice before the Giants made a first down. They drove 75 yards on 14 plays, then started at the Giants' 23 after Mike Haynes's interception. But Los Angeles settled for two field goals by Chris Bahr. The Giants stayed close enough for Simms to put them ahead 7-6 with his 18-yard touchdown to wide receiver Lionel Manuel midway through the third quarter.

It was still 7-6 early in the fourth quarter, when the Giants lined up at their 37, third-and-4. "Four yards and a first down would have been just fine," said guard Billy Ard, who led Morris on a sweep to the right. Even that looked unlikely when Ard ran into "a pile of people," as he put it. "There was nowhere to go," Ard said. "I thought the play was stopped. And then somebody hit me from behind and I banged into someone. The next thing I knew, Joe was sprung."

The guy who hit Ard from behind was Morris, making his own hole. Morris didn't stop again for 52 yards—until he was pulled down at the Raiders' 11. A Simms-to-Manuel encore on the next play made it 14-6.

The Raiders drove back for a field goal with 5:48 to play, but the Giants didn't let them have the ball again until the last 1:41. However, with Allen missing, the versatility of the Raiders' offense was missing, too.

Jim Plunkett of the Raiders not only winced, he fumbled, as Giants linebacker Andy Headen sacked him in New York's 14-9 victory. The Giants recovered two fumbles by Plunkett, both ending Raiders scoring threats.

Center Bart Oates (below) put Raiders defensive end Howie Long on his back, as Phil Simms looked downfield. Simms threw for 239 yards and two touchdowns, both to Lionel Manuel (above), who juggled, then caught, this scoring pass of 18 yards.

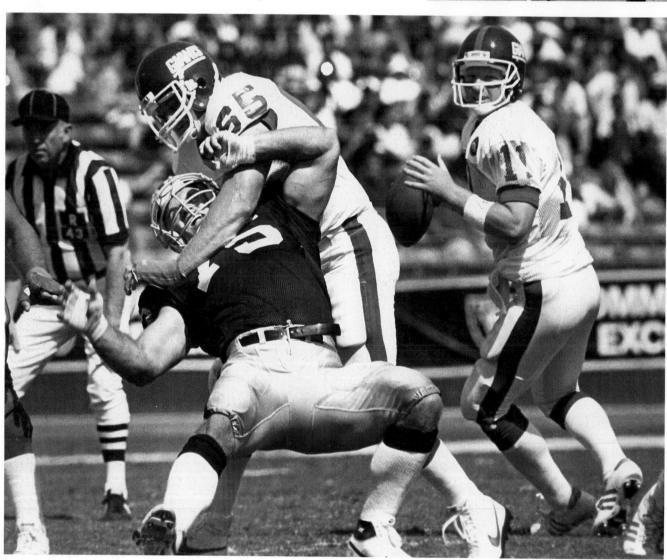

The Giants led 7-6 in the fourth quarter when Joe Morris (below) raced 52 yards down the right sideline to the Raiders' 11 to set up the touchdown that proved decisive. When the Raiders had the ball, they often ran into linebacker Carl Banks (above), who had 13 tackles.

A REBOUND VICTORY
Giants 20, Saints 17

t took a while to appreciate this one. There's something about struggling to beat the New Orleans Saints 20-17 at home that doesn't touch off madcap celebrating on the way to the parking lot. But this was more than a close call that should have been a breather. It was a W that could have been an L.

"It wasn't pretty," coach Bill Parcells said, "but in recent years, if the Giants got down by 17 points, it was usually all over." Matter of fact, the Giants hadn't overcome that big a deficit since 1970. "I'm starting to get the idea that we think we're supposed to win," Parcells said.

Early in the second quarter, the Giants had a tempting hand to fold. They were down 17-0. Their best runner, Joe Morris, had stayed home because of an allergic reaction to medication for a broken nose. Their best receiver, Mark Bavaro, was on the bench with a chipped tooth and what the team feared was a broken jaw. Their best deep threat, Lionel Manuel, injured his left knee in the second quarter, and it was feared the injury might keep him out for the season.

And the Saints were marching as proudly as the VFW in a Veterans Day parade. Their third of-fensive play was wide receiver Eric Martin's 63-yard touchdown catch of a pass from quarterback Dave Wilson, who was playing in place of injured Bobby Hebert. The Giants' next two drives ended with interceptions near midfield, the Saints cashed in, and it was 17-0 just 2:13 into the second quar-ter. But, as badly as they were outplayed, the Gi-ants trimmed that lead to 17-10 when Bavaro caught Simms's third-and-13 pass for a 19-yard touchdown just 80 seconds before halftime.

New York dodged another bullet when an illegal block on the second-half kickoff return wiped out Saints rookie Rueben Mayes's 100-yard touchdown.

Mark Collins's subsequent punt return for the Giants wasn't much of a return, except for the novel detail that he finished it without his helmet. And that after he stopped moving forward, Saints linebacker

Glen Redd smashed him head-to-head. Redd was wearing a helmet. Collins, with a concussion, col-lapsed on the bench six plays later. "I had tears in my eyes," said linebacker Harry Carson, who had greeted Collins on the sideline. "I think the guy who hit him, hit him on purpose. I got rededicated to play harder, and so did the others."

The drive ended with Raul Allegre's 28-yard field goal that cut the deficit to 17-13. That was it for the longest time. The lead didn't turn around until Simms's third interception and two penalties put New Orleans on the Giants' 26, third-and-1 and driving to clinch the victory. The Saints had momentum, but the Giants had a winning team's comfort that every play is a big break waiting to happen. On this one, Wilson turned the wrong way for a handoff, and Mayes ran into him. The ball fell loose. Defensive end Leonard Marshall claimed it for the Giants.

If the resulting 72-yard drive was a foregone conclusion, its climax was not. Tight end Zeke Mowatt had gone into the game without an NFL catch since 1984, when he led the Giants with 48. His knee injury in the last preseason game of 1985 was the kind that ends careers. He battled back onto the roster, but not into the lineup. Bavaro—in his second season—had the tight end job secured. His seven catches against New Orleans gave him the NFC lead with 25, and he trailed the yardage leader by only 14. But it was Mowatt's fourth catch that beat the Saints. His four-yard touchdown put the Giants ahead 20-17 with 8:03 to play.

The Saints had one more chance. They went three and out, again. For the second half, the Gi-ants held New Orleans to 8:41 in possession time, 13 net yards and one first down—on a penalty. Now it was the offense's turn to help. It kept the ball for the last 7:16.

"That was especially gratifying," nose tackle Jim Burt said. "We didn't have to go back on the field. We came back from adversity two weeks in a row now, and that's the sign of a mature team."

The New Orleans Saints were a much improved team in 1986. Ask the Giants, who fell behind 14-0 when rookie running back Dalton Hilliard went over every-one to score on this 1-yard dive.

The Giants had to scramble all afternoon against the Saints, which is exactly what Phil Simms (below) did against linebacker Rickey Jackson. Although Simms led a rally that produced a 20-17 victory, the Giants lost wide receiver Lionel Manuel (right), who went on injured reserve after suffering a hyperextension of his knee, following a tackle.

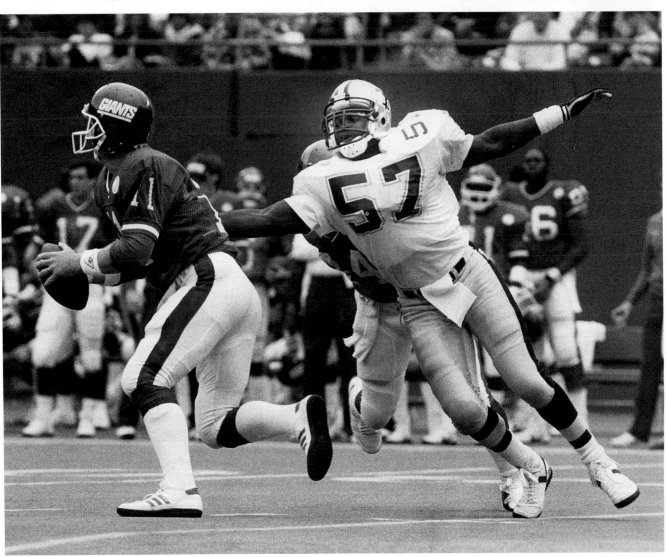

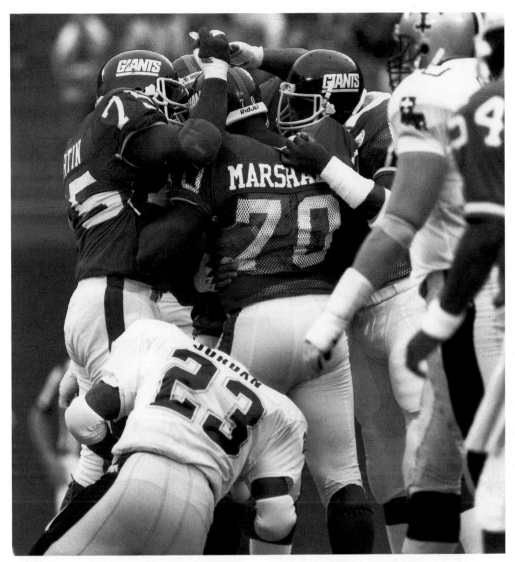

The Giants still trailed 17-13 when defensive end Leonard Marshall (left) recovered a New Orleans fumble on the New York 28 to earn a hug from his teammates. The offense immediately marched 72 yards to score on 4-yard pass from Phil Simms to tight end Zeke Mowatt (below, left). Saints defensive end Bruce Clark, meanwhile, had seven solo tackles in his team's defeat and sent a message to Madison Avenue on his shoes.

SOMETHING SPECIAL

Giants 13, Cardinals 6

A month earlier, he had been too slow to beat out the Giants' younger wide receivers. He always had been too small, only 5 feet 9 inches and 163 pounds. Still, it took the Giants only four games to realize how much they needed Phil McConkey. He never did much more than returning and covering kicks, but he showed them right away how the grubby work can win games.

There was nothing glamorous about the Giants' 13-6 victory at St. Louis. "The defense could have done this by itself," center Bart Oates said. It practically did. Leonard Marshall, Carl Banks, and Lawrence Taylor had two sacks each; the Giants had a total of seven. Kenny Hill's interception set up the Giants' 55-yard drive for their only touchdown. Banks's sack ended St. Louis's late drive to first-and-goal at the 6, and when the Cardinals got the ball back in good field position, Taylor forced a fumble that Hill recovered.

But Oates overlooked the unit that really won the game. "Thank God for my punter, my field-goal kicker, and my return man," coach Bill Parcells said of Sean Landeta, Raul Allegre, and McConkey.

McConkey had been waived in preseason and picked up by Green Bay. He played four games with the Packers, then was traded back to the Giants for an eleventh-round draft choice in 1987. He took injured wide receiver Lionel Manuel's place on the roster, but he really was replacing the punt-return men who had gained 34 yards on nine tries. He more than doubled their yardage with seven returns for 85 yards. His 20-yard return in the second quarter set the Giants up at the Cardinals' 34 for the 44-yard field goal that made it 3-3.

Field goals had been another problem after Ali Haji-Sheikh's latest injury. The Giants tried Bob Thomas in the first game and Joe Cooper in the next two before Allegre arrived to go 4 for 4 against the Saints and the Cardinals. His 31-yard kick, 39

seconds before halftime, provided a 6-3 lead the Giants never gave up.

And punting? "When they punted, they always gained position," St. Louis head coach Gene Stallings said. Landeta's 47.9-yard average on nine kicks was 9.9 yards better than the Cardinals got from Evan Arapostathis.

With eight first downs, the offense wasn't up to any long drives. It gained 61 yards rushing and 83 passing. The Giants' 10 kick returns outgained the offense by eight yards. Even their 55-yard touchdown drive was made possible by the Cardinals' Lionel Washington, who got a 32-yard pass interference penalty at the 1.

"You take the win and enjoy it, but we're not kidding ourselves," Oates said. With Joe Morris back at halfback, the Giants had planned to put on an infantry show against the winless Cardinals' twenty-fifth-ranked defense against the run. The Giants' 4-1 start was their best since 1968, but that team had finished 7-7. "We know what it feels like to play a good football game," Oates said. "We just haven't done it yet."

The victory came down to a favorable ruling in the instant-replay booth. St. Louis receiver J.T. Smith's catch in the end zone could have tied the game with barely three minutes left, but side judge David Parry ruled that one of Smith's feet had hit the sideline. Five minutes later, replay official Art McNally, the NFL's supervisor of officials, decided the replays were inconclusive.

McConkey's competitiveness, overcoming his size and speed, always had fueled him when told he couldn't play with the big guys. "It was just throwing oil on my competitive fire," he said. He was always the kid who practiced catching balls by diving into snowbanks in Buffalo, his home town.

"To be a kick returner is something that goes back early in my life," McConkey said. "It's a desire, a feeling inside that eleven guys are trying to take your head off. That's what drives you. Some guys don't like that. I do."

Although they won their fourth in a row, the Giants struggled again, slipping by St. Louis 13-6. Phil McConkey, waived in preseason and traded back to New York before the game, provided a big lift, returning seven punts for 85 yards.

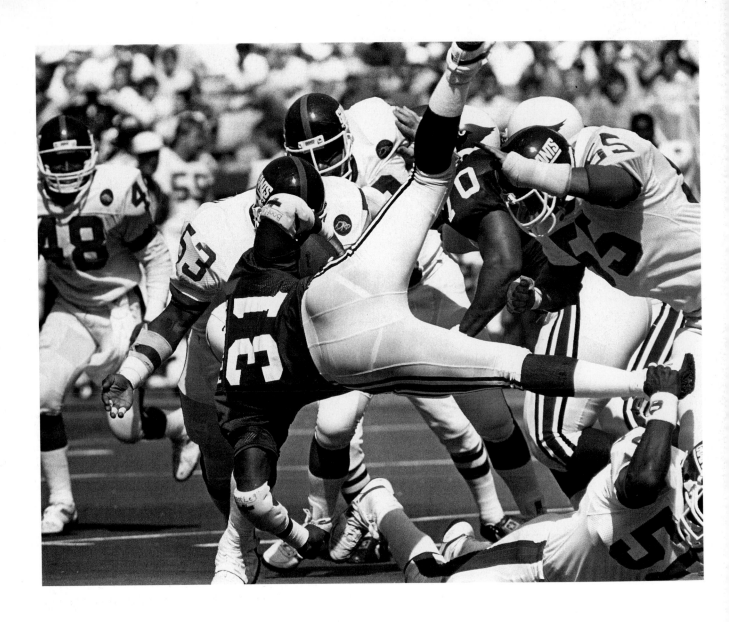

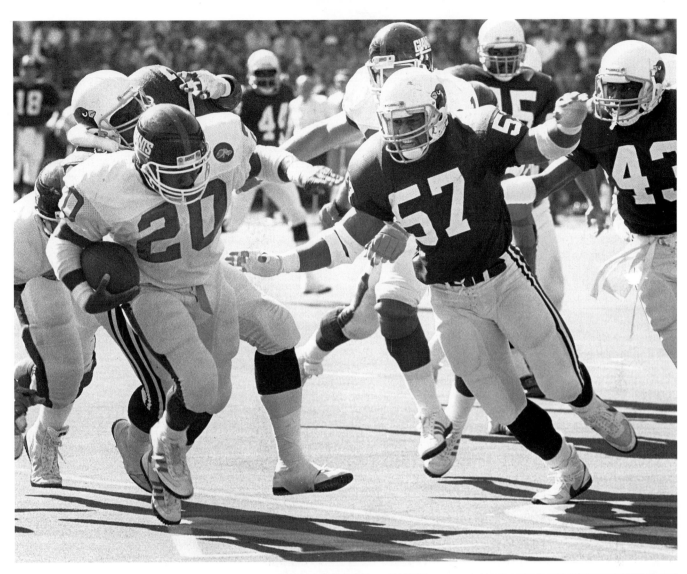

Cardinals running back Earl Ferrell (left) goes flying as linebacker Lawrence Taylor (on the ground) grabs him by the ankle. The Giants held St. Louis to 83 rushing yards. New York's Joe Morris (above) found running difficult, too, gaining just 53 yards on 17 carries. Vai Sikahema (right), the Cardinals' rookie punt returner who led the NFC in punt returns, took one back 61 yards against the Giants to set up a field goal.

FINALLY, A LANDSLIDE
Giants 35, Eagles 3

On the flight back from St. Louis a week earlier, nose tackle Jim Burt and coach Bill Parcells agreed the Giants had just played their four best defensive games in Burt's six seasons. The trouble was, they still hadn't put on a show, a rout that would dominate the Sunday night sportscasts. Winning 14-9 and 13-6 doesn't make people do double-takes. The Giants needed more than that before other NFL players started using phrases such as "a Giants-type defense" and "almost as tough as the Giants."

Wait until their future opponents got a load of their 35-3 whipping of Philadelphia in week six. Think they could bear to watch? The game snowballed into the kind of avalanche great defenses create. The Giants stuffed the run, set up some early short touchdown drives, and made the Eagles pass into their blizzard of blitzers. "They were attacking the line of scrimmage, coming after people," said Eagles coach Buddy Ryan, a voice of authority on defenses. "That's the way you play defense."

Philadelphia ran for 59 yards, but if you took away two quarterback scrambles and a first-half clock killer, it had 14 carries for 25 yards. Six runs on the first three possessions gained seven yards. So much for running. Eagles backs ran only five times for six yards in the second half.

When the game was in doubt, Leonard Marshall's sack at the Eagles' 10 set up the first touchdown drive, 34 yards. Lawrence Taylor's sack at the 2 set up the second one, 18 yards. Taylor also hurdled a blocker for a sack when the Giants led just 7-0 and Philadelphia was on the New York 5 after Evan Cooper's 58-yard punt return. The play kept them ahead 7-3 when Philadelphia was forced to kick a field goal.

In all, Taylor matched his career high with four of the six sacks. He was in on 13 tackles and later was named NFC defensive player of the week.

The Eagles netted minus-7 passing yards through three quarters. They gained 65 of their 117 yards on a meaningless fourth-quarter drive. Three of their nine first downs came on penalties.

"I can't remember one game in fourteen years when I had this many people around me," said Eagles quarterback Ron Jaworski. "I was getting hit every time I had the ball."

After giving up 31 points in the opener, the Giants had allowed 42 in five games. They'd held four of those opponents to less than 10 points. They hadn't given up a touchdown in 11 quarters. With their first five-game winning streak since 1970, the Giants tied Washington at 5-1 for first place in the NFC East.

Joe Morris started the offensive assault with a 30-yard scoring sweep behind fullback Maurice Carthon and guard Chris Godfrey. "That took a lot of pressure off a lot of people," quarterback Phil Simms said of the icebreaking score early in the second quarter. "It helped us get going." Simms, who completed 20 of 29 passes, scored next for the Giants on his first touchdown run in six years.

The second half began with the Giants' longest drive of the season, 80 yards in 14 plays. Solomon Miller's 10-yard touchdown catch was his first in the NFL, giving New York a 21-3 lead. Lee Rouson's first NFL touchdown came later, on a short pass that gained 37 yards. Elvis Patterson's first 1986 interception set up the other second-half touchdown at the Eagles' 21.

Halfback Ottis Anderson reached 8,000 yards in career rushing in his first game with the Giants, who had pushed him around the previous week when he was wearing a Cardinals' uniform. "It's a different feeling here," he said. "These guys know what it takes to win."

The frivolity peaked with Harry Carson's first NFL touchdown catch. The eleventh-year linebacker had scored twice on defense, but this time, he was a wingback on the field-goal squad. Holder Jeff Rutledge's 13-yard pass to Carson made it 28-3. As Carson said, "We had a lot of fun today."

Giants defensive end Leonard Marshall leaped to celebrate a sack of Eagles quarterback Ron Jaworski. Marshall had two sacks, and linebacker Lawrence Taylor four in New York's impressive 35-3 victory.

A GAME OF ERRORS

Seahawks 17, Giants 12

Statistics don't win games. Plays win games. A team can prance and preen all over the field all day, bringing the crowd to its feet and the opponent to its knees, but if it doesn't make enough plays that get into the end zone, it won't win the game.

The Giants knew that. When they went to Seattle, they knew it the way a child hears he shouldn't touch an oven. On the long flight back home, they knew it even better. They'd been burned.

"We did everything but score," offensive coordinator Ron Erhardt said after the Giants' 17-12 defeat knocked them out of a first-place tie in the NFC East. They outgained Seattle 307 yards to 218. With Joe Morris running for 116 yards, their advantage on the ground was 162-72. They had 22 first downs to 13.

The defense held Seattle running back Curt Warner to his poorest yardage total of the season, 56 on 19 carries. "It felt like half that," Warner said. "I was hit hard and often, and everything I got was extra difficult. That is the best, toughest defense I've seen in this league."

But that great, tough defense couldn't stop the Seahawks on third-and-8 from the Giants' 17 when Seattle led only 10-9, when as Jim Burt said, "The difference between a field goal and a touchdown was the difference in the game." Warner gained 12 yards on Dave Krieg's pass, then scored from the 1 for a 17-9 lead with 10 minutes to play.

The Giants' offense drove to the Seahawks' 22 or beyond five times, but the drives produced only three field-goal attempts, and one was missed. The other two drives ended with interceptions.

"We were very generous," said Phil Simms, who threw four interceptions. "I was, anyway."

In all fairness, Simms spent far too much of the game on his back. He took seven sacks. Pro Bowl left end Jacob Green had four, and two of them derailed drives after Seattle had taken a 17-9 lead.

Immediately after Warner's touchdown, the Gi-ants drove from their 10 to Seattle's 7. Bobby Johnson, whose sore ankle had limited him to four catches all year, suddenly caught three for 49 yards. Then, at the 7, Green dumped Simms on first down and the Giants had to settle for a Raul Allegre field goal.

New York forced a punt, got the ball at its 34 with 2:24 left and drove to the Seahawks' 22. Enter Green again, and a sack for minus-4. On fourth-and-14, cornerback Dave Brown intercepted Simms's pass at the 10.

Sacks had been a sticky issue in Seattle all week. The group that set the club record with 61 in 1985 had come crawling out of the gate with only nine in six games. The linemen were frustrated, and infuriated by the criticism. "I guess that brought up the intensity level to play a little harder," Green said.

Simms's first interception, also by Brown, set up Seattle's first-quarter touchdown drive of 43 yards. Seattle's 7-0 lead made the Giants' cumulative score 3-30 in seven first quarters. But they led 9-7 at halftime on Solomon Miller's 32-yard touchdown catch and Allegre's field goal.

The most costly interception was an eye-level pass that fullback Maurice Carthon tipped up and 6-foot 5-inch Seattle linebacker Bruce Scholtz intercepted. It put the Seahawks on the Giants' 19, and Warner made it 17-9 five plays later. "I just missed it," Carthon said. "No excuses."

Not that Carthon could be blamed for the loss. Three plays before Brown's closing interception, Miller dropped a pass that looked like a certain touchdown. And in the second quarter alone, Bart Oates's wide snap caused a missed extra point, an interception wasted Leonard Marshall's sack and Carl Banks's fumble recovery at Seattle's 25, and Terry Kinard's interception at the Seattle 25 led only to a field goal. In the third quarter, the Giants reached Seattle's 19, lost yardage on three consecutive plays, and missed a 42-yard field-goal try.

"Lots of ifs in the game," Oates said. "They made their ifs. We didn't."

The Giants' five-game winning streak came crashing down in Seattle, where defensive end Jacob Green (79) sacked Phil Simms four times in the Seahawks' 17-12 victory. Simms was sacked seven times in all and threw four interceptions.

DIVIDED ATTENTION
Giants 27, Redskins 20

At the end, the cheering matched the action. It hadn't always. The fans at Giants Stadium on this Monday night had been cheering huddles, men in motion, even a long catch by the visiting team. The game had the eerie sense of a sound track gone wacky.

"At first we were baffled," defensive end George Martin said. "We didn't know what was going on. Then somebody noticed a lot of TVs and radios in the stands. Being football players, we put two and two together and figured it out."

Of course! It really *was* a sound track mix-up. The fans were cheering another game. The New York Mets were winning the seventh game of the World Series 20 miles away...and in countless laps and earphones throughout Giants Stadium.

The divided enthusiasm didn't set well with some of the Giants. After all, this was their biggest game of the year. They were going to either tie the Washington Redskins and Dallas Cowboys for first place or fall two games behind, and their fans had the nerve to watch them take a 20-3 lead out of the corners of their eyes. "If they wanted to watch baseball, they should have gone to the baseball game," tackle Brad Benson said.

The World Series ended just as the Redskins were making a game of it, pulling within 20-17. Soon, it was 20-20. With the warm-up act over, the fans settled down to watch the thrilling end to the 27-20 victory. They saw the offense, of all things, pull it out for the defense.

"Give them a lot of credit," Giants linebacker Gary Reasons said. "They put the points on the board." After Washington tied the score, the offense got the ball with 3:58 to play and drove 81 yards. Joe Morris ran for 66 of them, including the 13-yard touchdown with 1:38 left.

Lawrence Taylor had three of the Giants' four sacks for 37 yards. He outgained the Redskins' rushing game by five yards. So the Redskins had

to pass...and pass...and pass. Jay Schroeder completed 22 of 40 passes for 420 yards. He had five completions of 35 yards or more. Wide receiver Gary Clark had three of those long catches, and 11 in all for 241 yards and a score.

The passing yardage was the most the Giants had yielded since 1980. On the other hand, if they could win when the defense played so poorly, was it too brash to cue up "The Impossible Dream"?

Morris kept the ball away from Schroeder for long stretches. He ran 31 times for 181 yards.

The Giants started off with Morris gaining 33 on a 57-yard field-goal drive. They went ahead 10-0 when Morris totaled 48 on an 80-yard drive that ended with his 11-yard score. Raul Allegre's 44-yard field goal at the halftime gun and Bobby Johnson's diving, 30-yard touchdown catch after Perry Williams's interception made it 20-3.

But five minutes later, with nearly 19 minutes remaining, it was 20-17. Ricky Sanders's 71-yard reception to the 1 set up one touchdown for the Redskins, and Clark's 42-yard catch scored another. Allegre missed a 29-yard field goal early in the fourth quarter. Then Max Zendejas struck with a 29-yard field goal with 4:06 to go, cashing in on a 47-yard pass to Art Monk and two third-down catches by Clark.

Of the winning drive, Simms said, "We got in the huddle, and all I said was, 'They're going to blitz. We know it. Let's go.' And sure enough, they blitzed on every play. We had some very good calls for that."

One was Johnson's 14-yard gain on third-and-10 from the Giants' 40. Another was Morris's draw play on first-and-20 two snaps later. "I was hoping they'd send in the draw," Simms said of the play-calling coaches. Morris started right, then went left and gained 34 yards down the sideline to the Redskins' 22. Three plays later, he scored. The season was halfway over with the Giants in first place—and the Mets world champions of baseball.

Joe Morris penetrated the Redskins for 181 yards and two touchdowns as the Giants created a three-way tie for first in the NFC East with a 27-20 victory over Washington. Morris's 13-yard scoring run with 1:38 left won the game.

Washington came into the game all alone in first place and didn't go quietly. Jay Schroeder (below) passed for a career-high 420 yards, while defensive end Dexter Manley (right) had two of the Redskins' four sacks of Phil Simms.

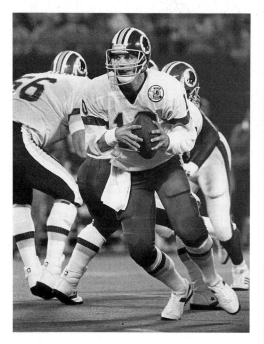

Running back Tony Galbreath (above) boosted the Giants' offense with 54 yards on five catches. However, the Giants Stadium crowd spent much of the game listening to radios and watching television sets describing the New York Mets' seventh-game battle in the World Series. When the Mets won, the scoreboard flashed the news.

MORRIS DOUBLES 181

Giants 17, Cowboys 14

This was the day the fever grabbed Giants fans by the throats. They couldn't stop yelling. By the fourth quarter, they were roaring. The Giants were defeating their second division title contender in two weeks. Either that, or they were blowing a late lead to the Cowboys for the second time this year. That wasn't the cure the afflicted fans wanted.

"The crowd was a factor," defensive coordinator Bill Belichick said. So was George Martin, the aging and cagey left defensive end. On Dallas's last-ditch drive, Martin drew three penalties against backup tackle Phil Pozderac, tipped a pass, and sacked the Cowboys out of field-goal range. Poor Pozderac couldn't hear the snap count, so he didn't start blocking until Martin started charging. Martin didn't stop charging until the final score shone radiantly from the scoreboard: Giants 17, Cowboys 14.

This, remember, was when the Cowboys still were a menace. They went into the game tied for first with the Giants and Redskins, both of whom they had beaten. No one knew they would win just one more game. No one even knew the Giants had shoved them toward oblivion by leaving running backs Tony Dorsett and Herschel Walker limping and by putting quarterback Danny White in a cast.

White, the leading passer in the NFC, broke his right wrist late in the first quarter. More precisely, linebacker Carl Banks broke White's wrist, sacking him at the Giants' 42 and liberating the ball for Jim Burt to recover.

The Giants were hurting, too, with wide receivers Lionel Manuel and Stacy Robinson on injured reserve. Phil Simms's 67 yards on a 6-for-18 passing day were his fewest for a full game since his first start as a rookie. He had one completion in the last 38 minutes, none on eight first-down passes.

That left the offense up to Joe Morris, who wouldn't have been turned away from an emergency room himself. Morris had carried 31 times six days earlier for 181 yards, his second-best NFL output. Now he matched the 181-yard total in 29 carries, six of them for 10 yards or more. He scored both of the Giants' touchdowns. He broke Eddie Price's club career record for 100-yard games with 11.

"I don't think I can do this the rest of the year," Morris said. "I didn't take a single hit that was punishing, but 29 carries make the tackles accumulate. We might have to do something different next week."

On the Giants' first touchdown drive, Morris had to run on seven of their 13 plays for 53 of their 69 yards. His eight-yard draw play restored their lead at 10-7. His six-yard touchdown run made it 17-7 with 12:14 to play after Gary Reasons's rush forced a six-yard punt to the Giants' 38.

But Dallas pulled within three points on Dorsett's 23-yard draw play with 7:29 left. "Andy Headen was blitzing and ran right by Dorsett," coach Bill Parcells said. "Sometimes that happens." And sometimes, as the Giants well knew, the Cowboys turn fourth-quarter leads into irrelevant memories.

Dallas actually gained 119 yards on its last drive, which began on the Cowboys' 16 with 3:33 to play. Most of them didn't count. Two of Pozderac's penalties—for holding and a false start—nullified 30-yard passes to the Giants' 6 and 11. The noise not only bothered Pozderac, it also kept Steve Pelluer, who took over for White, out of the Dallas Spread (Shotgun) formation, where he said he could have seen his receivers better.

Maybe the Shotgun could have stopped Martin from making the play of the game, but Pozderac nearly tackled him, drawing a yellow flag. With 37 seconds left, Martin sacked Pelluer for a 14-yard loss to the Giants' 41. The Cowboys had to attempt a tying field goal from 63 improbable yards.

"There aren't any bigger plays than that," Harry Carson said of Martin's heroics. Unlike at Seattle, the Giants were making them.

For the second week in a row, Joe Morris led the Giants past an NFC East contender, 17-14 over Dallas. And for the second week in a row, little Joe ran for 181 yards and scored twice.

The Cowboys defeated the Giants in the season opener, but Dallas made too many mistakes the second time around. Among the frustrated Cowboys was Rafael Septien (right), who missed all three field goals he tried. Dallas also lost three fumbles, including this one (below) by Herschel Walker.

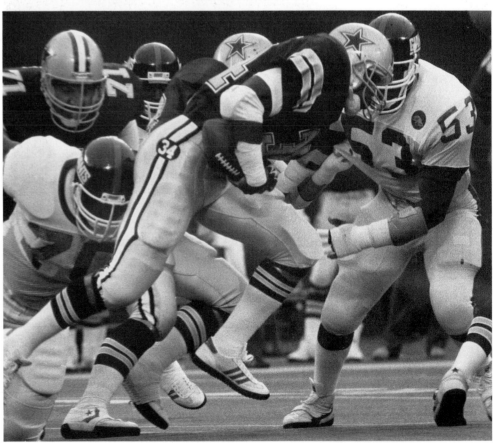

Giants linebacker Carl Banks (58) and his teammates put the squeeze on Dallas quarterback Steve Pelluer. The Giants sacked Pelluer and Danny White six times, including two by Banks.

A WIN IS A WIN, BUT...

Giants 17, Eagles 14

The frustrating thing was, the Giants had Philadelphia in full retreat. The Eagles were tripping over the guys behind them and scattering to sound the claxon, shred the game plan, or whatever it was teams do when they're about to become blots on the carpet.

But the Giants still hadn't gotten the hang of crushing a beaten opponent. At Philadelphia, the Giants took prisoners. They almost paid for it when the Eagles put together a late uprising. New York's 17-14 victory wasn't secure until veteran running back Tony Galbreath smothered an Eagles onside kick with 37 seconds to play.

"We can't keep winning this way," fullback Maurice Carthon said. "Good teams put the other clubs away when it's 17-0. We haven't gotten to that point yet. Hopefully we'll get there."

The Giants had 25 minutes left when they went ahead 17-0. They already had four sacks and two interceptions. They had contained the Eagles' offense with 44 net yards and six first downs. Philadelphia's quarterback, Ron Jaworski, was hurt. Joe Morris was well on his way to his fourth consecutive 100-yard game, a team record, and Phil Simms had passed for 130 yards.

Maybe it wouldn't have been so exasperating if New York's other pro football team hadn't been making the end zone its easy chair. The Jets seemed to score more often than John Madden said "Boom!" They were 9-1, averaging 29.8 points in an eight-game winning streak. The defending NFL champions' head coach, Chicago's Mike Ditka, was calling *them* the best team in the league. The Giants were being upstaged by their own stadium tenants, and all because the Giants were better at snuffing scores than igniting them.

The biggest play a quarterback made at Philadelphia was blocking a punt. Jeff Hostetler, a Giants' third-stringer, lined up at right end and the Eagles' John Spagnola forgot to line up across from him. Against a 10-man team, Hostetler blocked

John Teltschik's punt at Philadelphia's 48. Six plays later, Morris's 18-yard run made it 7-0.

Cornerback Elvis Patterson helped set up the Giants' other two scores. Patterson had lost his starting job to rookie Mark Collins for four games, but he was back in the regular defense after Collins separated a shoulder in the first quarter. His interception at the Eagles' 35 led to Raul Allegre's 22-yard field goal on the last play of the first half. On Philadelphia's first possession of the second half, he tipped a pass linebacker Gary Reasons intercepted at the Eagles' 36 and returned to the 18. Morris scored five plays later from the 3.

After that, the Giants made one first down. Simms was 0 for 3. Morris added only 29 of his 111 yards. The defense cooled off, too. If Eagles wide receiver Mike Quick hadn't moved illegally before his apparent 23-yard touchdown catch on a fake field goal, the Giants might have blown more than a chance to win big.

Quick redeemed himself the next chance he got, with a 75-yard touchdown pass from quarterback Randall Cunningham, and the Eagles had nearly nine minutes to make up 10 points. "That really let them back into it," nose tackle Jim Burt said. On the drive that let them further back into it, Lawrence Taylor's roughing-the-passer penalty canceled safety Herb Welch's interception, and linebacker Byron Hunt's pass-interference penalty put the ball on the Giants' 1. But only 45 seconds remained when Cunningham's touchdown made it 17-14.

The Giants' defense regained its NFL sack lead with seven, 40 for the season. Leonard Marshall had 2½, and Taylor's three gave him the league lead with 14½. The defense also notched another quarterback on its belt, although Jaworski's season-ending finger injury came merely from hitting his passing hand on a helmet.

The Giants' 8-2 record, tied with the Bears and Redskins for the NFC lead, was their best since their last conference championship in 1963.

Quarterback Jeff Hostetler was willing to do anything to help the Giants, even play on special teams. This block of John Teltschik's punt in the second quarter set up a Joe Morris touchdown as New York nosed out Philadelphia 17-14.

THE BIGGEST 'W'

Giants 22, Vikings 20

Close wins aren't always a drag. When a hobbling offense suddenly drops its crutches on a longshot, last-gasp drive, it can be exhilarating. When that drive survives fourth-and-17, it can turn a season around.

"That catch was probably the difference between winning the division and being the wild card," Bobby Johnson said later. The catch was his, 22 yards to the Minnesota 30 on fourth-and-17. Three plays later, Raul Allegre kicked his fifth field goal, 33 yards with 12 seconds to play, and the Giants were 22-20 winners instead of 20-19 losers. "I mean, you just don't make a fourth-and-seventeen," Johnson went on. "If we had lost that game, I think we'd have been pretty down. As long as I live, I don't think I'll catch another one like that."

The Giants overcame a Vikings' offense that gained 353 yards and a Vikings' defense that overloaded the strongside, daring New York to pass. No wonder. In the previous two games, Phil Simms's 14-for-36 passing had gained 197 yards. Wide receivers had caught three passes and were getting to be known as the "Blue Law" gang: never open on Sunday. In four games, Simms had produced three touchdown passes and seven interceptions.

Minnesota's defense did what it set out to do, holding Joe Morris to 49 yards. "It was a perfect time for us to have a big game," said Johnson, who gained 79 yards on four catches. They did. The passing game grossed 310 yards. The Giants sputtered inside the 20, where five drives added up to only four field goals and an interception, but at least their defense was making the Vikings settle for three-pointers, too. The Giants led 9-6 at halftime.

New York's only touchdown, Johnson's 25-yard catch, put the Giants ahead 19-13 with 9:30 to play. But, seven plays later, Minnesota's Anthony Carter caught a 33-yard touchdown pass from Wade Wilson, who took over after starting quarterback Tommy Kramer jammed his thumb. Minne-

sota still led 20-19 when the Giants got the ball at their 41 with 2:14 to go.

On the first play, wide receiver Stacy Robinson, just back from four weeks on injured reserve, dropped a long sideline pass that might have been a touchdown. On the second play, Simms dropped the Shotgun snap. He picked it up and flipped it more like a Frisbee toss to Johnson for 10 yards.

On the fifth play, Vikings defensive end Doug Martin (brother of the Giants' George) sacked Simms. It was fourth-and-17, Giants at their own 48, 1:12 to play.

During the time out, the coaches called "Half Right 74," with Robinson wide left, Johnson wide right, and Phil McConkey in motion toward Johnson. McConkey ran downfield inside Johnson. Cornerback Issiac Holt went with him. Johnson saw Holt's move and knew it would free the right sideline. He broke to it. Free safety John Harris moved toward Johnson, but not immediately. Simms never looked to his left. Pass rusher Mike Stensrud was getting close. He knew he had to loop the ball over Holt. Stensrud didn't let him see if he did it.

Johnson waited. And waited. He said he wanted to come back to meet the ball, but "I was afraid I might lose the first down." All the time, Holt was getting closer.

"I'd say if I threw the thing 100 times, I'd get it in there about five or six times," Simms said. "But when I let go, I knew I had a chance." The crowd told him he made it.

Allegre still had his job to do. He'd been almost as reliable as a light switch, 12-for-13 inside 42 yards, but he still hadn't quite felt part of the team. This helped. "Now I feel like I've made a contribution," he said. "I prepare myself all week for situations like this. It's just like taking a test."

The Giants were 9-2 for the first time since 1962, and half a game in first place until Washington won on Monday night. "They were excited," coach Bill Parcells said, "because the race is on. It wasn't on last week. It started for us today."

Wide receiver Bobby Johnson scored on this 25-yard catch-and-run in the fourth quarter to give the Giants a 19-13 lead over the Vikings. When New York fell behind 20-19, Johnson made a fourth-and-17 catch with a minute left for a first down on the drive to the field goal that won the game.

CLOSE, BUT WINNING

Giants 19, Broncos 16

Along with everything else, Bill Parcells probably started reaching for his phone before it rang. The players must have gotten their neckties just right on one try. New checkout lines no doubt opened at the market just as they wheeled up their grocery baskets.

Parcells could have had them run on third-and-21 from their own 18. With 1:35 to play and the score tied, it would have made sense. Denver would have had to use its last time out. Sean Landeta, with a 48.8-yard punting average, would have deposited the Broncos well beyond midfield.

"Bill thought about it for a moment and almost called a running play," said Phil Simms, who heard the coaches' time-out discussion. "But at the last minute, he said, 'Nah, forget the run. Let's try the Double Seam.'"

Why not? A team that made it on fourth-and-17 the week before surely could make third-and-21. The Giants did it, of course. They also gained 46 yards on second-and-13 to the Denver 15. Then, naturally, Raul Allegre made his fourth field goal, 34 yards with six seconds left for their 19-16 victory.

As Parcells said, "You've got to go with your gut feeling."

Third-and-21 was nothing compared to the play that kept the Giants within reach until the end. That was George Martin's sixth touchdown at defensive end, extending his NFL record. Martin's 78-yard interception return took 17 seconds and gave the Giants a 10-6 lead 43 seconds before halftime. Along the way, he broke quarterback John Elway's tackle at his own 45, leapfrogged Sammy Winder at the Denver 15, faked a lateral somewhere in between, stopped, started, bobbed, weaved, changed directions, and used a stiff-arm or two.

Just before Martin caught the ball, Denver was on the Giants' 13, driving for a 13-3 lead. Elway faked a handoff and lofted a short pass to running back Gerald Willhite, circling to the right. "The ball came and it surprised me," said Martin, who was looping toward Elway from left end. Martin, barely halfway from Elway to Willhite, leaped. The 6-foot 4-inch former Oregon basketball player reached back with his right arm, juggled the ball, brought it under control, and took off.

"I was flabbergasted," Elway said. "I didn't think I'd have any trouble getting the ball over his head." Parcells called it, "one of the greatest plays I've ever seen in football."

It was the Giants' only touchdown. Denver's defense gave up Joe Morris's sixth 100-yard game, but took away tight end Mark Bavaro, who had just one catch for 15 yards.

So the Giants adapted. They'd been doing that all year. It was their third game in five weeks against a first-place team, the third time they were outgained (405 yards to 262 this time), and the third time they won.

They weren't disappointed to see Elway leave town. His career-high 29 completions on 47 attempts gained 336 yards, and he led Denver rushers with 51. "I've never seen anyone like him . . . never," Lawrence Taylor said. But Elway didn't beat the Giants. He got the Broncos past the goal line only once, after Allegre's second-half field goals of 45 and 46 yards made it 16-9. Elway was 5 of 6 for 63 yards on the drive that made it 16-16 with 1:55 left.

Then it was time for Double Seam. The play sent receivers upfield along the yardage numbers, in the seams between the pass-coverage zones. Bobby Johnson gained 24 yards to the Giants' 42. Two plays later, from the 39, the Giants ran it again. This time, the Broncos faked a two-man blitz, knowing the Giants' adjustment would be a quick pass too short for a first down. The Giants didn't buy it. When Phil McConkey saw one of the blitz fakers drop back, he knew Simms had time to throw long. His leaping catch at the Broncos' 15 set up Allegre's game-winner.

As the Giants Stadium crowd cheered, defensive end George Martin (75) rumbled into the end zone at the end of his 78-yard run with an intercepted pass from Denver Broncos quarterback John Elway. It was New York's only touchdown in a 19-16 victory.

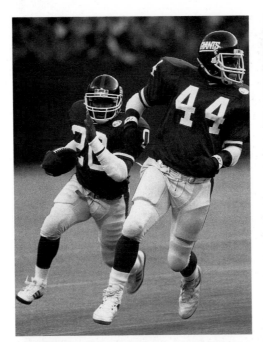

Quick-footed John Elway (below) drove the Giants crazy all afternoon, passing for 336 yards and scrambling for 51 more. Joe Morris (above left) had another 100-yard rushing day, following blockers like fullback Maurice Carthon for 106 yards. Phil Simms (right), who was sacked three times by the Broncos, checked to see if his lips were bleeding after one tackle for a loss.

Giants kicker Raul Allegre sailed into the air after his 34-yard field goal gave New York a 19-16 lead with just six seconds left. It was his fourth field goal of the game and ninth in two weeks.

SIMMS-SATIONAL!

Giants 21, 49ers 17

The Giants were going to need more than a couple of thrilling field-goal drives to scare defenses away from the line of scrimmage. Their 58-minute offense still was Joe Morris and a cloud over the passing game. The best teams could beat that. They could stuff the running game like a turkey and score points, too. Minnesota had almost done it but didn't score enough. Minnesota wasn't one of the top teams.

San Francisco was.

The 49ers followed the formula to a 17-0 halftime lead. They crowded Morris, held him to two net yards on six carries, and controlled the ball more than 19 minutes. "They manhandled us up front," quarterback Phil Simms said. Joe Montana passed for 145 yards, and a Monday night TV audience began to think all this hullabaloo over the Giants was just another New York media hoax. "We haven't been out of any games since 1984," head coach Bill Parcells said, "although we were almost out of this one."

The 49ers needed one more big play to heave the Giants out on the curb and make the game their private party. They figured to get it, too. With the Giants far behind and running nowhere, the 49ers' pass rush would look like a subway emptying at 8:55 in the morning.

This was the game Simms became a winning quarterback. He had been a successful one for a few years, but it was rarely enough for New York fans. He still wasn't a winning quarterback, like Montana, Marino, and McMahon, one who could grab a game that was swirling down the drain and pull it out with the strength of his passing arm.

Not until the third quarter at San Francisco. In that quarter, Simms won an out-of-reach game and overdue respect. He completed seven consecutive passes for 175 yards on three drives, scoring two touchdowns and setting up a third at the 1-yard line. While the 49ers punted three times, the Giants drove 49 yards in 1:26, 71 in 3:36, and 71 in

2:49. Fifteen plays, 21 points. When they made the 21-17 lead stand up, 49ers head coach Bill Walsh called the loss "the toughest we've had since I've been with the team."

"It shows what a little intensity can do," Parcells said. "My guys are tough. They don't quit."

Mark Bavaro sure didn't. He started things rolling with a 31-yard gain on an eight-yard pass. He gained 18 after the first 49er hit him. He broke two more tackles. He didn't go down until at least five 49ers had climbed on. Two plays later, Morris took a short pass for a 17-yard touchdown and it was 17-7.

The next drive teetered at the Giants' 49, where Parcells made a decision on fourth-and-2. "I was trying to do something to win the game, to be aggressive," he said. "If that play doesn't work, we'd probably lose the game." The play was Morris's only long run, 17 yards over right tackle. Stacy Robinson's touchdown catch on the next play made it a new game, 17-14.

Wide receiver Robinson, the Giants' big hope when he came off injured reserve a week earlier, caught five passes for 116 yards. His longest play, 49 yards to the 1, set up Ottis Anderson's first Giants touchdown, the game-winner.

It looked as if the Giants would pull away when Perry Williams intercepted Montana's next pass and returned it to San Francisco's 39. But Bavaro, pinballing upfield again, lost the ball at the 6. The game stayed in doubt until the last minute, when linebacker Carl Banks tackled Wendell Tyler for a three-yard loss at the Giants' 20, and linebacker Andy Headen's ad-libbed blitz forced Montana's hurried incompletion on fourth down.

The Giants had won six games in a row, the last five by four points or less and the last three on passing-game heroics. But this was Simms's biggest day. His 27-for-38 passing performance gained 388 yards. More than that, he had lost the albatross—he was a winner now. He was becoming a sturdy foundation for dreams.

Joe Morris celebrated after his 17-yard touchdown catch finally got the Giants a score against the 49ers. New York trailed 17-0 at halftime, but rallied to win 21-17 as Phil Simms completed 27 of 38 passes.

WINNING TOUGH

Giants 24, Redskins 14

One nice thing about passing is, it can put some cushion in a victory. That appealed to the Giants, who had won six consecutive games with all the comfort of a church pew. When they passed to attack from the start, instead of to battle back, they made their biggest game all year their most decisive victory in the streak.

The 24-14 victory at Washington not only wrapped up the NFC East with everything but the bow, it also bode well for the future. It was their second straight win over a likely playoff team, and they won them with rushing totals of 13 and 74 yards.

"When teams go out and try to stop Joe Morris," running back Morris said, "Phil Simms is going to have a good game." This was no longer just hopeful bluster. It went without saying that the Redskins would concentrate on Morris, so the Giants passed on their first five first-down plays.

They scored first on tight end Mark Bavaro's 9-yard catch early in the second quarter. They led for all but 1:32 thereafter. That was how long Simms needed to guide them 81 yards after the Redskins made it 7-7 just 1:55 before halftime. The seven-yard touchdown pass to Bobby Johnson was the last of three consecutive completions in 30 seconds for 60 yards. Simms finished the game with three touchdown passes and 265 yards.

Simms wasn't the only gear in the passing machine that was no longer squeaking. He took most of the heat when the air game was fluttering, but it wasn't his fault receivers had dropped balls and pass rushers had harassed him. The Giants had allowed 40 sacks in the first 12 games, ranking twenty-first in the league. Washington's defense came into this game tied for fifth in sacks. Right end Dexter Manley led the league with 17½, including two of the Redskins' three sacks in the first game between the two teams.

It was left tackle Brad Benson's chore to keep Manley at a safe distance. "I've never gotten this much attention in my life," the nine-year veteran said before the game. "It's like I was a quarterback or something."

Benson got even more attention after he shut out Manley. "I feel like I've just sucked a bunch of raw eggs," Manley said. "That was the least pressure I've put on a quarterback all year." Benson was the first lineman ever named NFC offensive player of the week. Washington was the second straight top-10 sacking team the Giants held to one sack.

New York's defense made Washington's first home defeat an easier task than the final score would indicate. The Giants had four sacks, hurried quarterback Jay Schroeder nine more times, tipped two of his passes at the line, and intercepted six. Lawrence Taylor had three of the sacks, taking the NFL lead with 19½ as he continued his mastery of Washington. The Giants had won four of their last five games against the Redskins, with Taylor totaling 11 sacks, 50 tackles, three forced fumbles, and one fumble recovery.

The heavy rush didn't give Redskins receivers time to get past the Giants' deeper-than-normal zones. When Schroeder grew bored with short stuff to Kelvin Bryant, the stage was set for interceptions on three consecutive second-half possessions.

The biggest interception was linebacker Harry Carson's, on the play after placekicker Raul Allegre gave New York a 17-7 lead late in the third quarter. Carson intercepted, and, two plays later, wide receiver Phil McConkey tipped Simms's pass up and brought it down for a 16-yard touchdown. The Redskins drove back to the New York 12, but defensive end Leonard Marshall intercepted a pass linebacker Byron Hunt had batted. Washington didn't score again until only 3:20 remained.

The Giants finally had won the big game for supremacy in the NFC East. They'd won seven straight now, all but one over winning teams, and four of the last five on the road. Only the defending champion Bears could match their 12-2 record, and the Bears kept beating 4-9 teams by 13-10.

Giants tight end Mark Bavaro reeled in a 9-yard touchdown pass from Phil Simms for the first score in the critical 24-14 victory over the Redskins, who came into the game tied with New York for first place. Bavaro had five catches for 111 yards.

Joe Morris (below) burst through a small hole behind blocks by guard Chris Godfrey (61) and tackle William Roberts (66) as the Giants dominated the Redskins. Tackle Brad Benson (60, above left) controlled NFL sack leader Dexter Manley (72) all day, holding him to no sacks and only three tackles. Linebacker Lawrence Taylor (56, above right) sacked Washington's Jay Schroeder three times.

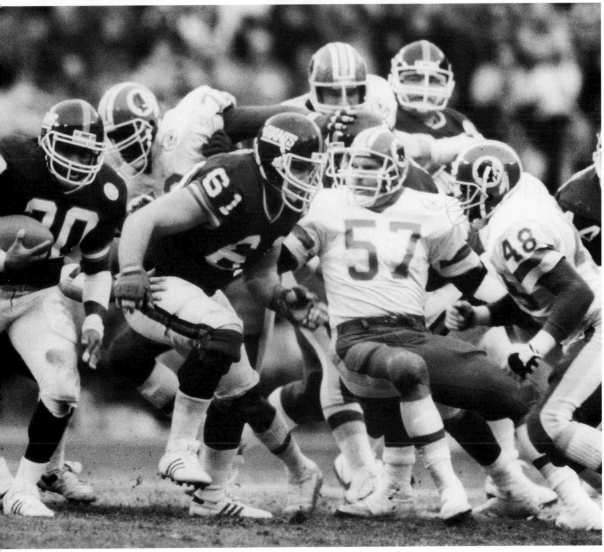

PUTTING ON THE STAMP

Giants 27, Cardinals 7

The division clinching would have been anticlimactic even if it hadn't actually happened Saturday evening when the Giants were at their hotel. They really had won the NFC East at Washington a week before. The Redskins' 31-30 loss at Denver in a Saturday game only made it mathematical.

But, as Carl Banks said, the Giants' 27-7 victory the next day made it official. "We had to put our stamp on it," he said. They left their cleat marks all over the Cardinals, too. Their nine sacks set a club record. Joe Morris's 179 rushing yards trailed the combined St. Louis offense by only five.

If the celebrating was subdued, it was because, as coach Bill Parcells said, "We still have more to do." First, they had to clinch home games throughout the playoffs. That would take another victory or a Bears defeat. "We want to say to everybody, 'This is my home. Come in and beat me in my home,'" Morris said.

The home-field goal also had its pragmatic side. In 1985, after the Giants defeated San Francisco at home in the wild-card game, Lawrence Taylor told Parcells, "Now I know the secret to getting into the Super Bowl. You have to play all your playoff games at home." That's what the Bears did in 1985.

Parcells made the St. Louis game a tune-up for the bad weather ahead. The Giants' passing game had flown briskly for two weeks now, so Parcells said, "I wanted to get the running game going." The Cardinals made it a good test, loading up on the line of scrimmage. "What you have to do is just keep pounding it," Parcells said, "knowing you're going to get some bad plays."

The Giants changed some blocking schemes. Instead of sending guards after strong safety Leonard Smith, the player designed to stay free for one-on-one tackles, they used quicker fullback Maurice Carthon and tight end Mark Bavaro. They wound up with 251 rushing yards, their season high. Morris scored all three touchdowns, set up two with

runs of 54 and 49 yards, and broke his one-year-old team record with 1,401 yards for the season.

The defense made the run emphasis work by keeping the ball close to the Cardinals' end zone. Six Giants possessions started at their 47 or beyond. Linebacker Harry Carson set up the first score with a sack at the Cardinals' 1-yard line. The 25-yard drive was the Giants' first touchdown all year in a first quarter.

St. Louis netted only 37 yards in the first half, when the Giants had seven sacks. They made five of the Cardinals' seven possessions finish behind where they had started. On one, shortly before halftime, the Giants backed St. Louis up 24 yards with three consecutive sacks. Raul Allegre's field goal with one second left made it 17-0 at the half.

The defense had a shutout against St. Louis until halfback Stump Mitchell threw a 15-yard pass to Roy Green with 6:37 to play. "I don't know that there's a team in the league that can stand them off," Cardinals head coach Gene Stallings said. "They whipped us every way possible. They're a Super Bowl team."

St. Louis made the Giants tinker with their pass rush, too. The Cardinals saturated the flanks against Taylor and Leonard Marshall, so the Giants got six sacks from men in the middle. They barely even noticed injured nose tackle Jim Burt's third consecutive absence. Jerome Sally had two sacks from nose tackle, and rookie backup Erik Howard added one. Quarterback Neil Lomax said it looked like "there were fifteen Giants out there against eleven Cardinals." Howard's sack was his first as a pro, as were rookie inside linebacker Pepper Johnson's two.

The division championship was the Giants' first since 1963. Even defensive end George Martin hadn't been around that long. He'd only been waiting since 1975. "It was twelve years of struggle and disappointment," he said, "and to see it finally pay off.... I just can't put it in words how it feels. But it's still too early to start celebrating."

Giants running back Ottis Anderson, an ex-Cardinal, faced his old teammates for the first time in New York's 27-7 victory over St. Louis. The Giants, who clinched the NFC East title when Washington lost the day before, won their eighth game in a row.

A 55-POINT WARM-UP

Giants 55, Packers 24

The nice thing about finishing with a cartwheeling, handspringing laughter was it gave the Giants a chance to take curtain calls. Everybody played. Five people scored the seven touchdowns. And after a 55-24 victory and a 14-2 season, the team's record book needed major revisions.

Beating Green Bay assured the Giants of staying home for all of their NFC playoff games. They weren't assured of playing more than one, but Gary Reasons said, "I think we're in the driver's seat now. Whoever comes in here, we're going to come out on top."

The Giants were undefeated at home, 8-0, for the first time since 1939. A nine-game winning streak tied the club record set in 1927 and matched in 1962. The 14 victories broke the club single-season record set in 1929 and 1930.

The 55 points against Green Bay were the most by the Giants since 1972. Their 448 yards and 30 first downs were season highs. Mark Bavaro set a Giants' record for tight ends with 66 catches and 1,001 yards for the season. Joe Morris's 115 yards boosted his club rushing record to 1,516 for the season.

The defense ranked first in the NFL against the run and second overall, climbing from eighth in the last four weeks. The Giants gave up more than 20 points for the first time since the opening game of the season, but, even so, only the Bears gave up fewer for the year. The team finished fourth in the NFL in sacks with 59, and Lawrence Taylor led the league with 20½.

"We were pretty shaky defensively in the second and third quarters," Bill Parcells said. "We have work to do." Coaches say things like that, but Parcells wasn't blowing smoke. The Giants nearly blew a 24-0 lead in the last five minutes of the first half, when Green Bay made it 24-17.

Nobody had to knock over furniture in the locker room. The players knew what was happening.

They remembered Philadelphia, where they nearly lost after neglecting to finish a team off. But they also remembered what they'd done since then. They were different now. "We didn't feel we were in trouble," quarterback Phil Simms said. "There was some reason why we scored twenty-four points. We just had to hang in there."

The defense forced a punt two minutes into the second half. Five minutes later, it was 31-17. Simms was 4 for 5 on the 80-yard drive. After Green Bay turned a 54-yard kickoff return into another touchdown, the Giants came right back. Simms side-stepped a sack and hit tight end Zeke Mowatt from the 22 for his third touchdown pass and a 38-24 lead. Defensive captain Harry Carson could have hoisted the Gatorade barrel right then, with 16:44 to play. The Giants got the ball three more times and scored three more times.

They could rest a week now. They would play the Rams or the 49ers in two weeks, and they honestly didn't care which one it was. The Giants had already beaten most of the best. They were confident the first playoff game would be just another domino, as would the Bears game they penciled in for the week after that.

"What we've done the last two, three years has been a learning experience," Carson said. "I think we've learned enough to realize we can win it all this year." It was a feeling shared from tight end Mark Bavaro to reserve running back Lee Rouson to the forty-fifth man. All three scored against Green Bay. Bavaro and Rouson had two touchdowns each. But the most gratifying play belonged to Tom Flynn.

Flynn had signed as a free agent only two weeks earlier, as insurance at safety after starter Terry Kinard went down. Midway through the first quarter, Flynn blocked a punt, caught the ball on the fly, and carried it 36 yards for the Giants' second touchdown, laughing all the way. Flynn had been cut by the Packers in November. A team going nowhere had told him he couldn't even tag along. Now he was going to the playoffs.

Joe Morris finished the regular season with a club-record 1,516 rushing yards, including 115 against Green Bay. The Giants won their ninth straight game, wrecking the Packers 55-24.

As they looked forward to the playoffs, Giants fans were aware their team had clinched the home-field advantage all the way through. The next away game—if the Giants made it—would be Super Bowl XXI in Pasadena, California.

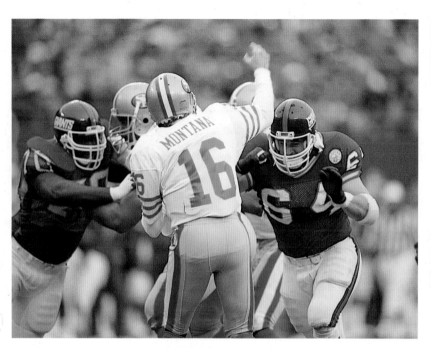

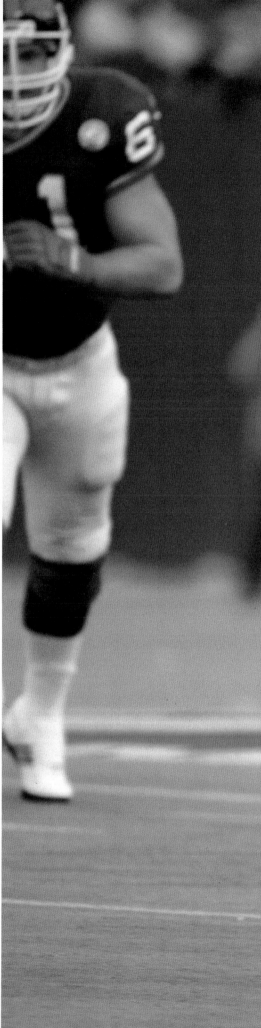

Late in the second quarter of the NFC Divisional Playoff Game, a crunching hit by nose tackle Jim Burt (64, above) put San Francisco quarterback Joe Montana out of the game with a concussion. On the same play, Lawrence Taylor intercepted Montana's pass and returned it 34 yards for a touchdown.

Joe Morris (right) ran for 159 yards against San Francisco, including a 45-yard touchdown. On the previous play, Herb Welch intercepted a pass from Montana and lateraled it to Elvis Patterson, who returned it 16 yards. Morris also scored on a two-yard run in the third quarter.

Midway through the first quarter of the NFC Championship Game against Washington, wide receiver Lionel Manuel was isolated against linebacker Monte Coleman (left). Manuel took full advantage of the mismatch, catching an 11-yard touchdown pass from Phil Simms to conclude an eight-play, 38-yard drive that gave the Giants a 10-0 lead on their way to a 17-0 victory.

Defensive end Leonard Marshall (70, above) and his cohorts made the NFC Championship Game a long one for Redskins quarterback Jay Schroeder. Washington's NFC Pro Bowl selection was sacked four times and intercepted once. He passed 50 times, completing only 20 for 195 yards.

In Super Bowl XXI, the Giants jumped ahead 7-3 the first time they had the ball. On a nine-play, 78-yard drive, Simms completed six consecutive passes. The sixth went six yards to backup tight end Zeke Mowatt (84, left) for a touchdown as a pumped-up Simms reacts.

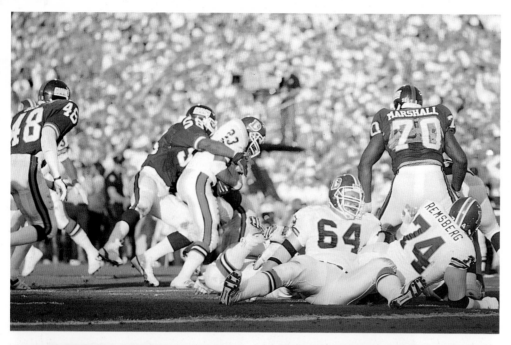

(Top) In perhaps the key defensive series of the game, the Giants stopped the Broncos after Denver had driven to a first-and-goal situation at the New York 1-yard line. On third down from the 3, Carl Banks (58) dropped Sammy Winder for a three-yard loss. On the next play, Rich Karlis missed a 24-yard field-goal attempt.

(Bottom) Late in the second quarter, on third-and-12 at the Denver 13, Broncos quarterback John Elway attempted to pass. New York defensive end George Martin chased Elway into the Broncos' end zone, where Martin sacked him. The safety cut Denver's lead to 10-9 at halftime.

The Giants took control on the opening drive of the second half. Simms capped the drive with a 13-yard touchdown pass to tight end Mark Bavaro (right), who looked up in thanks. The key play of the series was reserve quarterback Jeff Rutledge's one-yard run for a first down on a fourth-and-one situation at the New York 46-yard line.

Preceding page: Marshall (70) and Taylor (56) pressured Elway mercilessly throughout the second half. Denver failed to gain a first down in the third quarter, while the Giants scored 17 points to put the game out of reach.

Phil McConkey, a former Navy pilot, took to the air (right) in an attempt to score late in the third quarter. McConkey landed a yard short of his target. The play had begun with a handoff to Morris, who pitched the ball back to Simms. The Giants' quarterback then threw a 44-yard pass to McConkey. On the next play (below), with 24 seconds left in the third quarter, Morris took a handoff from Simms and followed the blocking of guard Chris Godfrey (61) for the touchdown that put the Giants ahead 26-10.

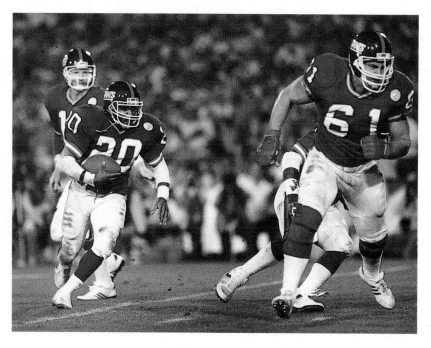

McConkey just missed scoring in the third quarter, but he went all the way in the fourth period (top, left). The Giants moved 52 yards on their first drive of the final quarter, scoring on a third-and-goal play from the Denver 6 as Simms's pass richocheted off Bavaro to McConkey.

How sweet it was! Morris and Taylor embraced as the clock wound down on the impressive victory (bottom, left).

Burt shared his moment of glory with his 5-year-old son Jim, Jr. They came out of the Giants' locker room to join a celebrating group of Giants fans.

Coach Bill Parcells's victory ride
(top) was the crowning moment
of an incredible season, while a
New York fan's license plate told
the story of the day.

THE PLAYOFFS

FROM A ROUT OF THE 49ERS THROUGH SUPER SUNDAY

A VERY BIG BANG
Giants 49, 49ers 3

This was more than just a dream come true. Who'd have been crazy enough to dream of winning 49-3? In the playoffs? Against the 49ers? The margins of 10 of the Giants' victories during the season added up to only 37 points. This was like dreaming for tickets to Hawaii and getting a Lear jet and a private island in the South Pacific.

In fact, it wasn't even considered outrageous to think the 49ers would win. They were healthy for the first time all season. They had beaten three playoff teams since the Giants burned them on Monday night. "We heard all week about how Bill Walsh never loses a game with two weeks to prepare," Joe Morris said.

The 49ers' fourth play of the game was a 50-yard touchdown pass. It looked that way, at least. Quarterback Joe Montana was raising his hands. Wide receiver Jerry Rice caught the quick slant-in at the 40. He was running up the middle with nobody in front of him...and what?! "The ball just popped loose," Rice said. No one touched Rice. He wasn't changing hands. He just dropped it. Rice and five Giants chased it into the end zone. Safety Kenny Hill recovered for New York.

Maybe there was something to this "team of destiny" talk after all. Hadn't the wind taken the Giants out of last year's playoffs, when the Bears went ahead on Sean Landeta's muffed punt? Now it was the Giants' turn.

It sold the Giants short to make a big deal of Rice's fumble. They had the kind of defense all year that could turn an early lead into a romp. Now, lately, they had developed an offense that could control the game and also strike quickly. True, an early touchdown could have sparked the 49ers. But 49 points' worth?

"I think we would have won anyway," Giants defensive coordinator Bill Belichick said. "We were ready to play today. It was very noticeable. The level of intensity was above what it normally

is. And that's understandable. We waited a year for this game. It was January 5, 1986, in Chicago that we all remember."

At 3 A.M. on the morning of January 4, 1987, guard Billy Ard said he woke up to a teammate's banging on the hotel walls. "Lots of guys were up, even the sound sleepers," he said. "We wanted it bad." In the locker room a few hours later, center Bart Oates said, "The electricity was incredible... there was an aura in here."

The Giants marched directly from Rice's fumble to a 7-0 lead, 80 yards in 10 plays. Phil Simms threw the touchdown pass 24 yards to Mark Bavaro, the first of three scoring passes to closely covered receivers. Simms threw four altogether, accounting for 96 of his 136 passing yards and tying a team playoff record. On three of the touchdown passes, Simms was rushed heavily. He was proud of that. "It means I stood in there as long as I could and got the job done," he said. That was the story of the Giants' season.

"Running the ball like we did at the beginning was the key for what we were able to do," Simms said. The Giants had run for only 13 yards a month earlier at San Francisco. "An embarrassment," Ard called it. New York hadn't been able to get around Carlton Williamson, the strong safety San Francisco parked at the line of scrimmage. This time the Giants used two tight ends. Both sides were strong, but committing two safeties to the run was more than the 49ers could do.

On his second carry, Morris gained 15 yards. He said he told himself, "Okay, maybe it's going to be a good day." In the second quarter, on a play he ordinarily ran to the right, Morris made it 14-3 with a 45-yard run to the left, away from Williamson. Morris finished the half with 116 yards, the game with 159. "We did just about everything we wanted to," Morris said.

So did the defense. It had only one sack, but that wasn't the idea against the 49ers. The Giants rarely even sent Lawrence Taylor. Montana throws

Whoops! Jerry Rice of the 49ers was sprinting away from New York's Harry Carson on his way to a 50-yard touchdown play early in the first quarter when he dropped the ball on the Giants' 27-yard line. In trying to pick it up, Rice kicked it into the end zone where New York's Kenny Hill recovered.

those quick, timing passes that beat the pass rush anyway, unless it comes up the middle and blocks his sight lines. On the play before Morris's 45-yard touchdown, linebacker Carl Banks was in Montana's face. The pass wobbled, and free safety Herb Welch intercepted it.

The game still could have gone either way until two minutes before halftime, when the Giants made the first of their two biggest plays. On fourth-and-6 from the San Francisco 28, they lined up to try a field goal. Then they shifted. Holder Jeff Rutledge became a Shotgun quarterback. Kicker Raul Allegre became a wide receiver. The 49ers didn't know Allegre had never caught a pass, even in high school. "You have to cover him," said Tom Holmoe, one of two 49ers defensive backs on the field. "Our punter, Max Runager, is a heck of an athlete. You never know." But on the other side, nobody covered Bavaro, who gained 23 yards and set up Bobby Johnson's 15-yard touchdown catch.

Two plays later, nose tackle Jim Burt led the best inside rush of the day, hitting Montana as he threw wildly to the left sideline. Taylor intercepted the pass at the San Francisco 34 and returned it for a touchdown. Just like that it was 28-3. "I think that took a little steam out of them," Taylor said.

It took Montana away, too. He spent the night hospitalized with a concussion. Burt felt bad about that. "Nobody respects Joe Montana more than I do," Burt said. "I hit him from the front. I couldn't pull up. He had no chance to get out of the way. I was worried I'd hurt him badly."

The 49ers finished with a total of 184 offensive yards, 196 below their NFC-leading average. They gained only 29 on running plays. With 16 seconds left in the third quarter, CBS began promoting next week's Giants-Redskins rematch for the NFC championship.

"Shattered," 49ers head coach Walsh said. "We were simply shattered. They played a perfect game. They destroyed our offense. The way they played, the only surprise would be if they don't win the Super Bowl."

The margin tied the third biggest in pro football playoff history. The only more one-sided games were Chicago over Washington 73-0 in 1940, and the Raiders over Houston 56-7 in 1969. It was San Francisco's worst loss since 1958.

"Hard to believe, wasn't it?" guard Chris Godfrey said. "I'll let myself enjoy it for a couple days. If we start thinking about the heights we've reached, we'll get out of the frame of mind we're in.

"I don't think it will happen. We're so steady a team. That's what Parcells thinks separates us from the other teams." That, and 46 points.

Joe Morris (above) picked up where he left off during the regular season by running for 159 yards and two touchdowns. Hyper-enthusiastic wide receiver Phil McConkey (right) accepted a pat on the back from running back Lee Rouson (22), after scoring on a 28-yard pass from Phil Simms that stretched the Giants' lead to 35-3.

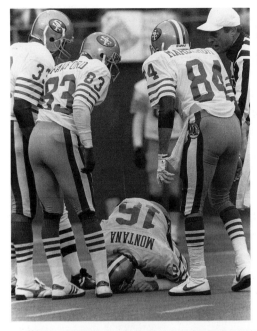

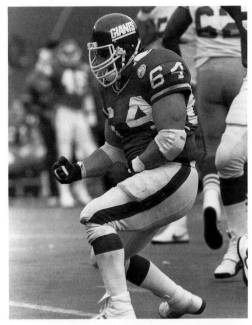

Anxious San Francisco players surrounded quarterback Joe Montana (top left), after he was dropped by a second-quarter hit by nose tackle Jim Burt. Montana left the game with a concussion. Burt (top right) celebrated his play, which forced Montana to throw wildly and led to Lawrence Taylor's 34-yard interception return (middle) for a touchdown and 28-3 halftime lead. Late in the fourth quarter, Giants coach Bill Parcells got his ritual Gatorade shower (below) to celebrate the victory.

CHAMPIONSHIP BLOWOUT

Giants 17, Redskins 0

The wind that really stung Washington was the blast of Giants pass rushers howling in quarterback Jay Schroeder's face. They put some color in his blockers' faces as they whooshed by. Harness the energy from that gale, and you could light up New York and New Jersey. Which, of course, the Giants did. When the game ended, with Jim Burt shaking hands with fans in the stands and Phil McConkey running laps around the field, the metropolitan area was aglow with good cheer.

"Somebody pinch me," Jerome Sally said after the Giants' 17-0 victory. Start spreadin' the news: The Giants were in the Super Bowl.

Sure, it was a gusty day for the NFC Championship Game. Most players called the 33-mile-an-hour wind the worst they'd played in. It was especially tough on the Redskins. But there was a reason for that. The Redskins had to pass more. If their running game had been able to outgain a blowing hot-dog wrapper, the wind might not have bothered them as much.

As Redskins safety Curtis Jordan said, "We got the ball for thirty minutes with the wind and thirty minutes against it, the same as them." The Redskins' problem was, either way, they had to go against the Giants' defense.

Schroeder said it was harder to pass *with* the wind. "It got on the tail of the ball and moved it wherever it wanted to," he said. "The receivers told me it was jumping around like a knuckleball."

The Giants took a quick 10-0 lead with the wind, but they weren't out of reach. The 49-yard drive that clinched the game in the second quarter was against the wind. Joe Morris scored from one yard. That same quarter, New York turned back two of Washington's four wind-aided drives past the Giants' 35.

At 17-0, the scoreless second half became equal parts countdown and balloon toss, with the Giants running on all but two plays and the Redskins passing 34 times in 35 snaps. "I think maybe they tried to throw too much when they had the wind at their backs," safety Kenny Hill said.

The Redskins hadn't run well against the Giants. They had gained 32 and 73 yards in their two regular-season meetings. George Rogers, their main earth shaker, had run 26 times for 52 yards. So this time, they made 262-pound guard Raleigh McKenzie their motion tight end, the guy who gets up a head of steam and bashes the nose tackle just after the snap. Burt, the nose tackle, expected it. When McKenzie came out for the first series, Burt clapped his hands in the huddle. "Good," he told his teammates eagerly.

By the time the Giants had a 10-0 advantage, the Redskins had tried three runs in two possessions. They had gained four yards. They finished with 40. Rogers gained 15 on nine carries. It was up to Schroeder.

Schroeder had to backpedal so far so fast, two of the Giants' four sacks were for 19 yards each. Lawrence Taylor had a thigh bruise for much of the game, so Carl Banks assumed his contract on the quarterback. "Our defense played like a school of piranha waiting for someone to stick their foot in the water," guard Chris Godfrey said. "They chewed them up." The Redskins, who were shut out for the first time since 1980, never crossed the Giants' 22.

Washington was 0 for 14 on third down, and 0 for 4 on fourth. "When you hold a team in that department to 0 for 18, it's not perfect, it's a miracle," coach Bill Parcells said. "You get those three-downs-and-punt series, it's artistic."

For the Giants, Phil Simms had ample time when he had to pass. The first touchdown was an 11-yard pass to Lionel Manuel on third-and-10. The big play of the second touchdown drive was 30 yards to Mark Bavaro on second-and-15. Both plays were crossing routes that couldn't come off quickly. Another third-and-20 pass to Manuel gained 25 on the first touchdown drive. It was his

Giants Stadium fans showered confetti on their favorites after running back Joe Morris's 1-yard touchdown run gave New York a 17-0 second-quarter lead over the Redskins. The Giants maintained that lead to win the NFC championship and a trip to Super Bowl XXI.

first catch since his knee injury in the fourth game.

Nobody laughed when Redskins head coach Joe Gibbs called the coin toss the key to the game. Parcells had decided at 7:15 A.M., when he arrived at Giants Stadium, to take the wind if he won the toss. Gibbs said he would have done the same thing. Guard Russ Grimm called tails for Washington, the coin came down heads, and the rout was on. Three plays and a 23-yard punt set the Giants up for Raul Allegre's 47-yard field goal. Three plays and a 27-yard punt set up their 38-yard touchdown drive. Both punters kicked into the wind four times, but Washington's Steve Cox averaged 28.8 yards to Sean Landeta's 42.3.

The wind helped stop the Redskins' first good drive in the second quarter. They were trying a 51-yard field goal when the wind fiddled with center Jeff Bostic's snap, causing the holder to fumble. "I think that was the biggest play of the game," said Banks, who recovered the ball at the Redskins' 49. And the Giants promptly capitalized with their last touchdown.

Washington's best chance followed Morris's fumble at the Giants' 37 with 1:44 left in the half. It ended on Parcells's choice for play of the game, when Taylor and Harry Carson stacked up Rogers on fourth-and-1.

Carson picked up the Gatorade barrel with 1:56 to play, right after Schroeder left the field with a mild concussion on his thirtieth and last incompletion. Parcells was ready this time. He squirted Carson with a water gun, then made a nice move to miss the full brunt of the shower. Carson got a worse dousing himself from Burt. "I hope it happens one more time," Parcells said.

"Today the New York Giants marched out of the dark ages," Morris said. "The only thing we used to hear was about the good old days. Now they're talking about us."

Twenty-three years of muttering about the Giants came to an end. Fans showered the players with confetti, toilet paper, newspapers, and affection. "This was our ticker-tape parade," Burt said.

Parades had been a hot topic all week. New York mayor Ed Koch said he wouldn't host a post-Super Bowl parade for a "foreign team," not with the $700,000 bill for security and clean-up. Soon, practically every suburban mayor in northern New Jersey was offering his town's streets for a Giants parade. Koch changed his mind when American Express agreed to pick up the tab, but the Giants had heard enough. They scheduled a celebration for Giants Stadium. "If we beat Denver," McConkey said, "you'll see some real celebrating. I ain't worried about no parade."

New York took advantage of a strong wind in the first quarter. When Washington's Steve Cox (above), under a heavy rush from Eric Dorsey (77), punted just 27 yards into the wind, the Giants drove 38 yards for a touchdown and 10-0 lead. Tight end Mark Bavaro (right) raced 30 yards with a Phil Simms pass to set up Morris's 1-yard touchdown.

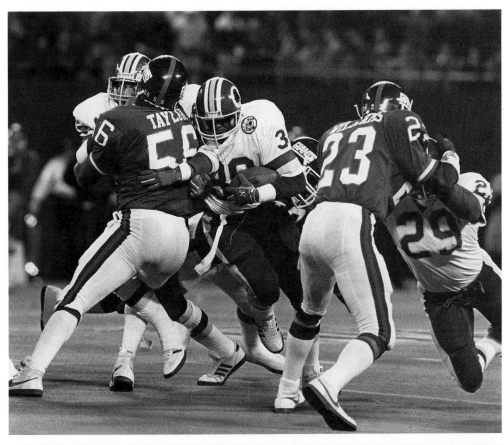

Washington's George Rogers (38, left) found tacklers such as Lawrence Taylor (56) in his way all day, as he gained just 15 yards on nine carries. Quarterback Jay Schroeder (below) had a frustrating game, too, even as the holder for a field-goal attempt. Center Jeff Bostic's snap sailed away from him. Carl Banks (58) recovered at Washington's 49-yard line, setting up the Giants' final touchdown.

NEW YORK PHIL

Giants 39, Broncos 20

Even before the game started, Phil Simms knew he was in for something special. His teammates saw it in his eyes. They saw it in his warm-up passes, too. Every one on the money. As Simms recalled later, "I told the guys after warm-ups, 'I've got it working. I've got the fastball.' "

Until then, Simms had been little more than a bit player on the Super Bowl stage. The Broncos had John Elway and the Giants had their defense, and Simms would just fill some time between the stars' acts. Elway, now *there* was a quarterback. He was tall, fast, strong-armed, handsome, outgoing. He had it all—Namath's arm with Tarkenton's elusiveness—and everybody knew he was the key to the game. He was the one guy who could bring the Giants down. "Phil didn't say anything," Jim Burt said, "but we all knew he didn't take it well, like he was saying, 'Hey, what about me?' "

Simms said the Elway hype didn't bother him. He had more to worry about than counting column inches in the papers. He had a secret, too. Simms's fastball was cooking long before pregame warm-ups. Two Fridays before the game, he was so hot, coach Bill Parcells told him to save some of it. "We knew all week he was going to have a big game," tight end Zeke Mowatt said.

Simms had a big game the way Everest is a big hill. His 88 percent passing, 22 for 25, didn't just set a Super Bowl record. It was the third-best performance of all-time in the NFL. In the second half, when the Giants' 30 points set a Super Bowl record, Simms was 10 for 10 and threw for two of his three touchdowns. His passes squeezed into openings like cab drivers in Manhattan traffic.

"In my wildest dreams, I couldn't have hoped it would work out this way," Simms said. "It's like when you're playing golf, and you know every putt's going to go in. I didn't throw one ball where I felt, 'Damn! I want that one back.' It's a good feeling being out there and when they call a play, you know you'll probably complete it. You don't know who to, but you know you will."

He also upstaged Superman. Elway had a good game, too, but this time, the leading man didn't get the girl. Simms walked off with the MVP award for his role in the 39-20 victory. "This dispelled for the last time any myth about Phil," Parcells said.

"This makes everything worth all the crap I've taken over the years," Simms said. He had taken more than his share from Giants fans who needed goat horns on which to hang their frustrations. They blamed him for shortcomings at receiver or on the line, and they didn't appreciate the big plays he did make. "He's not called upon to put up the big numbers all year," center Bart Oates said. "He's just called

upon to produce in critical situations." Simms was a quarterback who made the tough passes, took the necessary risks. That's what made his 88 percent all the more remarkable. He didn't throw for many five-yard gains into the flat.

When it was over, Simms decided he belonged with the best, after all. "I can't deny it anymore," he said. "I thought I was an all-right player, but this one was the big one for me to play well in." That night, he said, he couldn't keep from chuckling to himself. "I went up to my room with my family, and we sat around and smiled a lot," he said.

The thing that did bother Simms, going into the game, was how people still hadn't noticed the Giants' passing game. "I talked to the receivers all week and said, 'Look, nobody's giving us any credit. Let's just come out of the gates running and I'll get the ball to you.' " He also lobbied Parcells and offensive coordinator Ron Erhardt. He told them, "Let's don't run, run, ask me to pick up 10 yards on third-and-10, and wonder why I'm not in the game."

"We felt we had to come out and attack," Parcells said. The Broncos hadn't concerned themselves much with the pass in November, and that made it hard to run. So the Giants passed on 9 of 11 first downs in the first half. They completed all nine. The Broncos had to guess. That made it hard to play defense.

"They changed their whole offensive attack," Denver linebacker Karl Mecklenburg said. "Pass first, run second. It surprised us."

Simms was 6 for 6 on the Giants' first drive. His six-yard touchdown to Mowatt put the Giants ahead 7-3. But Elway was hot, too. Denver drove right back for a 10-7 lead, forced a punt, and stormed upfield to first-and-goal at the 1.

That was when the game started turning around. After three failed running plays, it was fourth-and-goal at the 6. The Broncos would have to settle for 13-7, except they didn't even get that when Rich Karlis missed a 23-yard field-goal attempt. By halftime, the Giants had cut the lead to 10-9 on George Martin's safety sack, while Karlis missed another field goal, from 34 yards with 13 seconds left.

The Broncos put their running game back in the trunk after the goal-line stand. It wasn't a big surprise. One of the reasons so much had been made of Elway was the Giants' run defense. It led the league in the regular season and held two playoff opponents to 34.5 yards a game, 1.9 per carry. But the Broncos had to offer at least a token threat on the ground. That was Elway's only hope of surviving the pass rush. In the Super Bowl, a team has to run before it can strut.

The Broncos barely could stagger. After Sammy Winder's four-yard loss on third-and-goal, Denver's backs showed one-yard rush-

It was a clear, sunny day in the Rose Bowl (above) as the Giants wore down Denver 39-20 in Super Bowl XXI. A crowd of 101,063 basked in warm 80-degree weather. Also enjoying the afternoon was Giants quarterback Phil Simms, voted the game's most valuable player. In the first quarter, Simms enjoyed excellent protection as he passed 17 yards to Mark Bavaro to set up New York's first touchdown, a 6-yard pass to Zeke Mowatt. For the game, Simms completed 22 of 25 attempts.

ing on nine carries. The Broncos passed on their next 22 plays and wound up with 52 yards rushing, 27 by Elway.

"It seemed like the halves were two different games," Denver center Billy Bryan said. Instead of taking a 20-7 lead at halftime, maybe finishing the Giants off, the Broncos only made them angry. The Giants scored a field goal and four touchdowns the first five times they had the ball in the second half.

"We felt confident at the half," Denver defensive end Rulon Jones said. "We were up in the game and our offense really hadn't been stopped." But the Giants felt pretty good, too. "We just calmed down and said, 'These guys have shot their wad, and we're only down by one point,' " Oates said.

Maybe the Giants went into the game too tight. They weren't themselves in the locker room, Phil McConkey said. They were usually so businesslike. They didn't even hoot and holler after they won the NFC championship. But today, McConkey said, "The guys were anxious to get out. We went to Mass this morning, and we couldn't wait for Father to start. We'd been waiting so long."

It had been a long week. For one thing, the Giants didn't like the way the pregame stories made it seem as if they could just pluck a victory off the shelf, like a cereal box. And they had a tough week of practice. The running and hitting and coaching insults Wednesday and Thursday were as intense as they'd been all year. "It paid off, didn't it?" Burt said later. "We were in the right mood."

As fate had it, the Rose Bowl public-address system was playing "New York, New York" as the Giants took the field after halftime. "I got goose pimples," said McConkey, who got the Giants' fans even more riled up as he led the Giants out pumping his fists in the air. The Giants outgained Denver 163 yards to 2 in the third quarter. "Everything we did was right," Simms said.

There was Jeff Rutledge's quarterback sneak on fourth-and-1, after the Giants lined up in punt formation. That kept the go-ahead drive alive on the Giants' first possession. Then there was the flea-flicker late in the third quarter. McConkey was turned upside down just short of the goal line after catching Simms's pass for 44 yards. When Joe Morris scored on the next play, the Giants led 26-10 and began to think they had this thing under control.

This time, when the Gatorade doused Parcells, it baptized all Giants fans with new hope, new pride. It washed away the bitterness from 30 years of memories, 30 years without an NFL championship, from Alan Ameche and sudden death in '58 and the blood streaming down Y.A. Tittle's face in '63 to the fumble, the airplane banner, and the ticket-burning protest of '78. "We buried all the ghosts tonight," Parcells said. "They're all gone."

When the game was over, at about the same time a jubilant conga line started moving up Second Avenue a continent away, Harry Carson remembered watching the first Super Bowl 20 years earlier. He remembered the Packers' Willie Davis and the Chiefs' Buck Buchanan. They were his heroes. He used to draw their numbers on his T-shirts. That morning, as he lay in bed with those thoughts, it hit him, "the realization that I'm playing in Super Bowl XXI and there are going to be kids across the country putting '53' on T-shirts, just like I was emulating Willie Davis and Buck Buchanan."

Let the rest of the world dream of the Giants for a change. Their dream finally had come true.

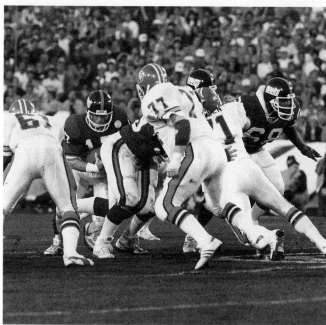

The Broncos dominated most of the first half, but only had a 10-9 lead at intermission as kicker Rich Karlis (above) missed two short field goals in the second quarter. This miss, from 34 yards, came with just 13 seconds left in the first half. Giants reserve quarterback Jeff Rutledge (below) sneaked for two yards and a first down at the New York 48 early in the third quarter. Five plays later, Phil Simms threw 13 yards to Mark Bavaro for the touchdown that put the Giants ahead for good.

Giants defensive end Leonard Marshall (above) sacked Denver's John Elway for an 11-yard loss on the last play of the third quarter. By then, New York had opened a 26-10 lead. In 1986, linebacker Harry Carson was as dangerous on the sideline as he was on the field. At the end of each Giants victory, he doused head coach Bill Parcells with a barrel of Gatorade . . . and Super Bowl XXI was no exception.

ADVANTAGE BRONCOS

Elway made the Giants uneasy right away. On the first offensive play of the game, he bailed out of the pass rush and resurfaced 10 yards upfield. "I thought, Uh-oh. Wear your track shoes. It could be a long day," outside linebacker Carl Banks said. "We expected him to scramble and pass. But we didn't want him to run."

Okay, pass it is. Elway threw his first on third-and-7. Mark Jackson gained 24 yards to the Giants' 39-yard line. The next pass gained five. The Broncos tried two runs from there. Already, running was an uphill battle. But they were close enough for Rich Karlis's 48-yard field goal. It tied the longest field goal in Super Bowl history, and it gave the Broncos a 3-0 lead after only 4:09.

If that's the kind of game they wanted, Simms could give it to them. He brought the Giants right back to a 7-3 lead. He passed for 69 yards on the 78-yard drive, including the touchdown. He overcame a holding penalty with an 18-yard strike to Stacy Robinson on third-and-10. "We loosened them up pretty quick," Simms said. "You hit a few passes and it kind of gets them thinking." A 17-yard pass to Mark Bavaro carried to the Broncos' 6. On the next play, Mowatt beat strong safety Dennis Smith crossing the end zone. Your turn, Denver.

It didn't take long. Ken Bell's 28-yard kickoff return put the Broncos on their 42, and three complete passes in a row moved them to New York's 24. Now the Giants were getting frustrated. After Sammy Winder's gain to the 24, Carson hit him out of bounds. The personal foul cost 12 yards, half the distance to the goal line. Taylor didn't like the call. He picked up the flag. *That* penalty, unsportsmanlike conduct, cost another half the distance, to the 6-yard line. "Everybody was somewhat nervous," Carson said. "Elway came out and made a couple plays. I was involved in a penalty. L.T. had a penalty that put them down in scoring range.

That was the thing that really hurt us."

On third-and-goal, Elway dropped back from the 4. He looked downfield. Then he ran straight ahead. He could have somersaulted for the touchdown. The quarterback draw surprised the Giants.

"We caught them in the perfect defense," Elway said. "They went from the 3-4 defense and walked their outside backers up to the line so it was five-on-five at the line." When Elway dropped to pass, the linebackers retreated into zones. All Elway had to do was go the opposite direction from the nose tackle, and he had a touchdown.

This was the sort of one-man show people expected from Elway. It was the sort of show some people thought could beat the Giants. When New York fell behind 10-7 with 2:06 left in the first quarter, Simms said, "I thought, God, for once these people might be right."

A small detail had gone largely unnoticed on the Giants' first drive. On Joe Morris's first carry, he turned the right corner for an 11-yard gain. His next carry picked up eight up the middle. Morris's running on the Rose Bowl's grass surface had become something of an issue during the week, mainly because of that 14-yard belly flop of a game in San Francisco. For the season, his 62-yards-a-game average on grass didn't quite measure up to his 95 on artificial turf. But this field was firmer than San Francisco's, more like the field on which he gained 110 against the Raiders. Morris's first two carries crossed his question mark off the list of Things That Might Make a Difference.

So much for the defensive struggle. In the first quarter, the two quarterbacks were 13 for 13. The quarter ended at second-and-11 for the Giants, after Ottis Anderson lost a yard. They punted.

It was early, though, and Parcells wasn't worried. "Everyone's pretty frisky there in the first quarter, including Elway," he said later. "I told our defensive guys before the game not to worry about him getting completions early and making plays. Just keep wearing them down."

Denver quarterback John Elway frustrated the Giants throughout the first half with his running and passing. On the game's first play, he dropped to pass, then scrambled for 10 yards.

CLOSE DOESN'T COUNT

Elway's most dangerous runs usually ended with passes. It was third-and-12 from Denver's 18 when he dashed out of the pocket and away from Taylor. His pass to Vance Johnson gained 54 yards. Two more third-down plays, and the Broncos were at the 1-yard line, first-and-goal.

The Broncos had gotten too close. Eleven yards to the end line wasn't enough space to stretch the Giants' zones. "We knew coming in that we couldn't entirely ignore the run," Elway said. "We felt we could run against them."

Denver went to its best runner on first down. Elway took off toward the right pylon. He could have passed. He said he saw Winder in the back corner of the end zone, but he decided to run. "I tried to cut inside Lawrence, but he has such great speed, we couldn't get to him [with a blocker]." Taylor, with help from nose tackle Erik Howard, stopped Elway at the 2. The Broncos were using three tackles and two tight ends. There would be no tricks. They tried to bulldoze the bigger Giants out of their way. On second down, Gerald Willhite went over right guard. Carson met him at the line.

On third-and-two, Banks remembered Denver's only touchdown at Giants Stadium had been a four-yard pitchout to Sammy Winder. "I expected that play again, and that's what they called." Winder headed left, away from Banks. But the Giants linebacker caught up with him. He didn't worry about looking good. He just stuck his helmet in Winder's way. "I had zigzags in my eyes the rest of the half," Banks said. Carson and cornerback Perry Williams finished off Winder at the 6.

"It really hurt when we didn't get in the end zone then," Elway said. "If you're looking for a turning point, that was it. Had we scored there, it might really have turned things around for us."

They not only blew the touchdown, they missed the field goal. Karlis, wide right from 23 yards, now had both the longest success and the shortest

miss in Super Bowl history. That miss might have changed the Broncos' thinking. When their next possession came to third-and-12 from their own 13, they went for the big play.

Before the Giants lined up, left end George Martin told nose tackle Erik Howard to ignore what he said at the line. He was going to pretend to call for a stunt. He wanted Ken Lanier, Denver's right tackle, to hear it. "The offensive tackle looked at me and thought he had a tip," Martin said. "As I came off the ball, I faked inside and he bit on it." Martin charged straight ahead, outside Lanier.

The inside rush was strong, too. It kept Elway from stepping up in the pocket. He kept retreating past the goal line. He stepped to his right, away from the inside rush. Martin was there. "And then," Martin said, "we embraced."

It was a safety. With 2:46 left in the half, Denver's lead had been pared to 10-9. "I had no way to get rid of it," Elway said. "There was nowhere to go inside or outside, nowhere to dump it."

Denver's defense held again, so the Broncos had a chance to get back some pride and some points in the last 1:05. They drove to the Giants' 16. But Karlis missed again, this time from 34 yards. The air was out of Denver's balloon.

"I really hurt the team," Karlis said, crying into a towel. He felt miserable. He knew better than to try to steer the ball instead of just kick it, but he had made that basic mistake in the biggest game of his life, and he felt it cost Denver the game. "I thought about all the people I let down," Karlis said. "I'm sorry. . . .I'm hurting."

Karlis's teammates encouraged him at halftime and absolved him after the game. "It wasn't Rich's fault at all," Johnson said. But there was no denying the misses were a dose of fresh air for the Giants.

"It gave us the feeling that we could go in at halftime, get back together, and come out and win the game," Mowatt said. "If he made those two field goals, it could have been Denver sitting here as world champs."

Momentum started to turn New York's way in the second quarter, when veteran defensive end George Martin sacked John Elway for a safety, trimming Denver's lead to 10-9.

OVER...AND OUT

The third quarter recalled the classic scene in *Raiders of the Lost Ark,* in which Harrison Ford patiently watched his nemesis do fancy sword tricks, then shot him. The Broncos had had their fun. Now it was time for the Giants to blow them away.

They needed a big gamble for a small gain to get them started. Their drive to open the half stalled quickly at their own 46. It was fourth down, two feet to go. Sean Landeta lined up in punt formation. But who was the blocking back? That was Jeff Rutledge, the backup quarterback. "They knew something was up," Parcells said, "but they didn't know what."

Rutledge moved up to the center. Now the Giants couldn't punt. Rutledge had two options: run a quarterback sneak or take a delay-of-game penalty, which would give Landeta more room to avoid a touchback. He waited. "I wasn't trying to draw them offside," he said. He was only trying to make the right decision. Rutledge was not supposed to run unless the first down was a sure thing.

With four seconds on the play clock, Rutledge looked to Parcells. Parcells nodded. "Their linebackers were five yards deep," Bart Oates said. "They couldn't stop us." Rutledge plunged over right guard for two yards.

The Broncos hadn't been entirely surprised. They kept their regular defense on the field. They remembered the first Giants game. That time, on fourth-and-5, the Giants handed off after shifting from punt formation.

"We were just trying to win the game," Parcells said. "This game is not for the faint-hearted. Every time I've challenged these guys with something like this, they've come through. And Rutledge is a real heady guy, perfect for making that decision."

The third quarter had belonged to the Giants all year. They outscored opponents 106-37 in the regular season and 21-0 in the playoffs. They outscored Denver 17-0.

The go-ahead touchdown was a third-and-6 play, 13 yards to Mark Bavaro with 10:08 left in the quarter. Smith covered Bavaro closely as he angled toward the left sideline, then back toward the goal post. But when the ball came, Smith didn't reach for it. "I probably shouldn't have thrown it, but I saw this little opening," Simms said. The Giants led 16-10.

Then they stopped Denver when three consecutive passes fell incomplete. "We seemed to suddenly get that electricity," Simms said.

Taylor had addressed the rest of the defense at halftime. He had not been pleasant. Elway had gotten the Giants out of their game since his first 10-yard run. They were almost afraid to rush him, Taylor said, as good as he was out of the pocket. "We were worried about the heat, the shoes. We were playing finesse defense," Taylor said. He told the other players that would not do.

"In the second half, we just went out and knocked their heads off," Taylor said. "In most games, the team that plays rough and tough will win out in the end. That's what happened today."

After Raul Allegre's 21-yard field goal and another three-plays-and-out series for Denver, the Giants led 19-10 late in the quarter. From Denver's 45, Simms handed off to Morris, who then turned and lateraled back to Simms. "We've run those flea-flickers in practice for I don't know how long, but never in a game," Simms said. He didn't see Bobby Johnson, who was open in the end zone. But he saw Phil McConkey.

"When I caught it," McConkey said, "I kept saying to myself, 'I'm going to score a touchdown in the Super Bowl.'"

He didn't. McConkey made it to the 1 before ex-Giant Mark Haynes sent him cartwheeling in the air. But Morris's one-yard run on the next play was almost anticlimactic. "When I hit McConkey," Simms said, "I thought, 'That's it. We've won it.'" With 24 seconds left in the quarter, the Giants led 26-10. Finally, they felt comfortable.

Tight end Mark Bavaro put the Giants ahead for good early in the third quarter when he knifed between Denver safeties Randy Robbins (48) and Dennis Smith to take a 13-yard touchdown pass from Phil Simms. The play gave New York a 16-10 edge.

GATORADE TIME

The losing coach always is the last to know. Denver's Dan Reeves didn't feel it slipping away until now. "We came out at the start of the fourth quarter," he said, "and all of a sudden we were second-and-twenty-five. That put us in a hole, and we never got out of it."

The Broncos were at their 5 when Elway threw his first pass of the fourth quarter. The inevitable finally happened. Elvis Patterson intercepted it. From their own 48, the Giants drove to a 33-10 lead with 11:56 to play.

Simms's six-yard touchdown pass was his poorest throw of the day. It was thrown so hard, it bounced off the top of Bavaro's chest and over his shoulder. "I don't know what happened," Bavaro said. "They hit me pretty good. I was kind of dizzy for a few seconds. Then I looked down, and there was McConkey with the ball."

McConkey had grabbed the rebound. He had his Super Bowl touchdown after all. Usually on that play, McConkey crossed the end zone from the right while Bavaro went from the left. But this time, he stayed on Bavaro's side. He just followed Bavaro. "At first, I was a little lost," he said. It didn't matter. The ball found him, and he caught it.

Elway wasn't finished. Beaten, maybe, but not finished. He threw five consecutive completions, setting up Karlis's 27-yard field goal with 6:01 to play. "He never gave up," said Banks, who led the Giants with 10 tackles. "Usually, if you give it to a quarterback, he's worrying about what you're doing. He gets it in his eyes. But he kept his composure and fought all the way."

"I don't want to play him anymore," Marshall said. The feeling was mutual. "That defense," Elway said, shaking his head. "That defense just seems to know what I want to do and how I'm going to try to do it. There's more quickness up front than we've seen. For this day, the Giants were definitely the best team in professional football."

The Giants' last touchdown, Ottis Anderson's two-yard run, made it 39-13 with 3:18 left. Allegre missed an extra point for the first time all season. Denver scored again, but Vance Johnson said he cried in the end zone after his 47-yard catch. He said he thought, "So what?" It was over.

Soon, Carson would borrow a security guard's yellow jacket, the better to sneak up on Parcells with a barrel of Gatorade. Carson drenched him twice. Tackle Brad Benson and guard Chris Godfrey carried the coach off the field in triumph.

Burt ran through the crowd that was taking over the Rose Bowl field. He shook hands and slapped palms. His jersey and shoulder pads were off, leaving only his undershirt. His index fingers pointed to the sky. His 5-year-old son, Jim, Jr., was on his shoulders. Burt had wangled him onto the sideline with four minutes to play. "I wanted him with me," he said. "He's my pride and joy."

Carson and Martin were in the locker room, resting tired old bones. Carson had waited 11 years for this, Martin 12. "It's been a long time coming," Carson said. "I loved every minute of this week."

Simms accepted the MVP award soaking wet. Oates and Benson had doused him with ice water. "The ultimate compliment," Oates said. "I think it was very appropriate to cool the guy down, as hot as he was in the game."

The Broncos barely grazed Simms all game. Toward the end, he told Taylor he might last a few more years. He finally understood how some quarterbacks could play so long. "You get on a good team, you don't get hit so much," he said.

But enough of the future. The future could wait. The Giants didn't let themselves get roped into talking about dynasties. They enjoyed the moment.

"We're the champions now...today," Taylor said. He thought about showing off his Super Bowl ring back home in Williamsburg, Virginia. "As long as I live," he said. "I'll always have a Super Bowl ring. One time in my career, we are the best in the world. That's the most important thing."

Everything went right for the Giants in the second half. Phil McConkey scored early in the fourth quarter when he caught Phil Simms's 6-yard pass, which bounced off Mark Bavaro's (89) shoulder pads.

APPENDIX

New York Giants, 1986

WELLINGTON T. MARA
President

TIM MARA
V.P.–Treasurer

RAYMOND J. WALSH
V.P.–Secretary

GEORGE YOUNG
V.P.– General Manager

HARRY HULMES
Asst. General Manager

BILL PARCELLS
Head Coach

2 RAUL ALLEGRE
Kicker

5 SEAN LANDETA
Punter

11 PHIL SIMMS
Quarterback

17 JEFF RUTLEDGE
Quarterback

20 JOE MORRIS
Running Back

22 LEE ROUSON
Running Back

23 PERRY WILLIAMS
Cornerback

24 OTTIS ANDERSON
Running Back

25 MARK COLLINS
Cornerback

27 HERB WELCH
Safety

28 TOM FLYNN
Safety

30 TONY GALBREATH
Running Back

34 ELVIS PATTERSON
Cornerback

44 MAURICE CARTHON
Running Back

46 GREG LASKER
Safety

48 KENNY HILL
Safety

51 ROBBIE JONES
Linebacker

52 PEPPER JOHNSON
Linebacker

53 HARRY CARSON
Linebacker

54 ANDY HEADEN
Linebacker

55 GARY REASONS
Linebacker

56 LAWRENCE TAYLOR
Linebacker

57 BYRON HUNT
Linebacker

58 CARL BANKS
Linebacker

 **59** BRIAN JOHNSTON *Center*
 **60** BRAD BENSON *Tackle*
 **61** CHRIS GODFREY *Guard*
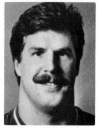 **63** KARL NELSON *Tackle*
 **64** JIM BURT *Nose Tackle*
 **65** BART OATES *Center*

 **66** WILLIAM ROBERTS *Tackle*
 **67** BILLY ARD *Guard*
 **68** DAMIAN JOHNSON *Tackle*
 **70** L. MARSHALL *Defensive End*
 **74** ERIK HOWARD *Nose Tackle*
 **75** GEORGE MARTIN *Defensive End*

 **77** ERIC DORSEY *Defensive End*
 **78** JEROME SALLY *Nose Tackle*
 **80** PHIL McCONKEY *Wide Receiver*
 **81** STACY ROBINSON *Wide Receiver*
 **84** ZEKE MOWATT *Tight End*
 **86** LIONEL MANUEL *Wide Receiver*

 **87** SOLOMON MILLER *Wide Receiver*
 **88** BOBBY JOHNSON *Wide Receiver*
 **89** MARK BAVARO *Tight End*
 BILL BELICHICK *Assistant Coach*
 ROMEO CRENNEL *Assistant Coach*
 RON ERHARDT *Assistant Coach*

 LEN FONTES *Assistant Coach*
 RAY HANDLEY *Assistant Coach*
 FRED HOAGLIN *Assistant Coach*
 PAT HODGSON *Assistant Coach*
 LAMAR LEACHMAN *Assistant Coach*
 JOHNNY PARKER *Assistant Coach*

 MIKE POPE *Assistant Coach*
 MIKE SWEATMAN *Assistant Coach*
 TOM BOISTURE *Dir. of Player Personnel*
 JERRY SHAY *Dir. of College Scouting*
 TIM ROONEY *Dir. of Pro Personnel*
 RAYMOND J. WALSH, JR. *Dir. of Research & Dev.*

Alphabetical Roster

NO.	NAME	POS.	HT.	WT.	BIRTHDATE	NFL EXP.	COLLEGE
2	Allegre, Raul	K	5-10	167	6/15/59	4	Texas
24	Anderson, Ottis	RB	6-2	225	11/19/57	8	Miami
67	Ard, Billy	G	6-3	270	3/12/59	6	Wake Forest
58	Banks, Carl	LB	6-4	235	8/29/62	3	Michigan State
89	Bavaro, Mark	TE	6-4	245	4/28/63	2	Notre Dame
60	Benson, Brad	T	6-3	270	11/25/55	9	Penn State
64	Burt, Jim	NT	6-1	260	6/7/59	6	Miami
53	Carson, Harry	LB	6-2	240	11/26/53	11	South Carolina State
44	Carthon, Maurice	RB	6-1	225	4/24/61	2	Arkansas State
25	Collins, Mark	CB	5-10	190	1/16/64	R	Cal State-Fullerton
77	Dorsey, Eric	DE	6-5	280	8/5/64	R	Notre Dame
28	Flynn, Tom	S	6-0	195	3/24/62	3	Pittsburgh
30	Galbreath, Tony	RB	6-0	228	1/29/54	11	Missouri
61	Godfrey, Chris	G	6-3	265	5/17/58	4	Michigan
54	Headen, Andy	LB	6-5	242	7/8/60	4	Clemson
48	Hill, Kenny	S	6-0	195	7/25/58	6	Yale
74	Howard, Erik	NT	6-4	268	11/12/64	R	Washington State
57	Hunt, Byron	LB	6-5	242	12/17/58	6	SMU
88	Johnson, Bobby	WR	5-11	171	12/14/61	3	Kansas
68	Johnson, Damian	T	6-5	290	12/18/62	1	Kansas State
52	Johnson, Pepper	LB	6-3	248	7/29/64	R	Ohio State
59	Johnston, Brian	C	6-3	275	11/26/62	1	North Carolina
51	Jones, Robbie	LB	6-2	230	12/25/59	3	Alabama
5	Landeta, Sean	P	6-0	200	1/6/62	2	Towson State
46	Lasker, Greg	S	6-0	200	9/28/64	R	Arkansas
86	Manuel, Lionel	WR	5-11	180	4/13/62	3	Pacific
70	Marshall, Leonard	DE	6-3	285	10/22/61	4	LSU
75	Martin, George	DE	6-4	255	2/16/53	12	Oregon
80	McConkey, Phil	WR	5-10	170	2/24/57	3	Navy
87	Miller, Solomon	WR	6-1	185	12/6/64	R	Utah State
20	Morris, Joe	RB	5-7	195	9/15/60	5	Syracuse
84	Mowatt, Zeke	TE	6-3	240	3/5/61	3	Florida
63	Nelson, Karl	T	6-6	285	6/14/60	3	Iowa State
65	Oates, Bart	C	6-3	265	12/16/58	2	BYU
34	Patterson, Elvis	CB	5-11	188	10/21/60	3	Kansas
55	Reasons, Gary	LB	6-4	234	2/18/62	3	Northwestern State, Louisiana
66	Roberts, William	T	6-5	280	8/5/62	2	Ohio State
81	Robinson, Stacy	WR	5-11	186	2/19/62	2	North Dakota State
22	Rouson, Lee	RB	6-1	222	10/18/62	2	Colorado
17	Rutledge, Jeff	QB	6-1	195	1/22/57	8	Alabama
78	Sally, Jerome	NT	6-3	270	2/24/59	5	Missouri
11	Simms, Phil	QB	6-3	214	11/3/56	8	Morehead State
56	Taylor, Lawrence	LB	6-3	243	2/4/59	6	North Carolina
27	Welch, Herb	S	5-11	180	1/12/61	2	UCLA
23	Williams, Perry	CB	6-2	203	5/12/61	3	North Carolina State

R—A first-year player who has not previously been in an NFL training camp.

How They Were Built

YEAR	DRAFT (27)	TRADE (5)	FREE AGENTS (13)
1975 5-9 4th, NFC East	DE George Martin (11)		
1976 3-11 5th, NFC East	LB Harry Carson (4B)		
1977 5-9 5th, NFC East			T Brad Benson
1978 6-10 5th, NFC East			
1979 6-10 4th, NFC East	QB Phil Simms (1)		
1980 4-12 5th, NFC East			
1981 10-8 3rd, NFC East	LB Lawrence Taylor (1) G Billy Ard (8C) LB Byron Hunt (9)		NT Jim Burt
1982 4-5 10th, NFC Regular Season	RB Joe Morris (2)	QB Jeff Rutledge (from L.A. Rams)	NT Jerome Sally
1983 3-12-1 5th, NFC East	DE Leonard Marshall (2) T Karl Nelson (3A) CB Perry Williams (7) LB Andy Headen (8) LB Robbie Jones (12A)		TE Zeke Mowatt
1984 10-8 2nd, NFC East	LB Carl Banks (1A) T William Roberts (1B) LB Gary Reasons (4B) WR Lionel Manuel (7)	RB Tony Galbreath (from Minnesota) S Kenny Hill (from L.A. Raiders)	G Chris Godfrey WR Bobby Johnson CB Elvis Patterson
1985 11-7 1st, NFC East	WR Stacy Robinson (2) C Brian Johnston (3B) TE Mark Bavaro (4) RB Lee Rouson (8) S Herb Welch (12)		RB Maurice Carthon T Damian Johnson P Sean Landeta C Bart Oates
1986 17-2 NFC Champions	DE Eric Dorsey (1) CB Mark Collins (2A) NT Erik Howard (2B) LB Pepper Johnson (2C) S Greg Lasker (2D) WR Solomon Miller (6A)	RB Ottis Anderson (from St. Louis) WR Phil McConkey (from Green Bay)	K Raul Allegre S Tom Flynn

Front Office

Wellington T. Mara . . . . President
Tim Mara . . . . V.P. and Treasurer
Raymond J. Walsh . . . . V.P. and Secretary
George Young . . . . V.P. and General Manager
Harry Hulmes . . . . Asst. General Manager
John Pasquali . . . . Controller
Ed Croke . . . . Director of Media Services
Tom Power . . . . Director of Promotions
Tom Boisture . . . . Director of Player Personnel
Jerry Shay . . . . Director of College Scouting
Tim Rooney . . . . Director of Pro Personnel
Raymond J. Walsh, Jr. . . . . Dir. of Research & Development
Victor R. Del Guercio . . . . Director of Special Projects
Jim Gleason . . . . Box Office Treasurer
Francis X. Mara . . . . Assistant to the President
John Gorman . . . . Asst. Box Office Treasurer
Jim Lee Howell . . . . Special Scout, Consultant
Jim Trimble . . . . Personnel Consultant
Jerry Angelo . . . . Scout
Rosey Brown . . . . Scout
Rick Donohue . . . . Scout
Greg Gabriel . . . . Scout
Ken Kavanaugh . . . . Scout
Chris Mara . . . . Scout
Ed Rutledge . . . . Scout
John Dziegiel . . . . Head Trainer Emeritus
Ronnie Barnes . . . . Head Trainer
John Johnson . . . . Trainer
Jim Madaleno . . . . Trainer
Tony Ceglio . . . . Video Coordinator
John Mancuso . . . . Asst. Video Coordinator
Ed Wagner . . . . Locker Room Manager
Ed Wagner, Jr. . . . . Equipment Manager
Joe Mansfield . . . . Field Security Manager
Dr. Russell Warren . . . . Team Physician
Dr. Allan Levy . . . . Assoc. Team Physician
Dr. Hugh Gardy . . . . Dentist
Joel Goldberg . . . . Director Career Counseling
Cy Fraser . . . . Halftime Director
Julius Horai . . . . Administrative Assistant
Ed Olivari . . . . Administrative Assistant
Vinny Swerc . . . . Administrative Assistant
Millie Bohan . . . . Secretary
Connie Brunetto . . . . Secretary
Paddy Fox . . . . Secretary
Janice Gavazzi . . . . Secretary
Rita Giordanetti . . . . Secretary
Kim Kolbe . . . . Secretary
Joann Lamneck . . . . Secretary
Madeline Meyer . . . . Secretary
Nilda Velez . . . . Secretary
Marianne Vogt . . . . Secretary
Andrea Wagner . . . . Secretary
Colleen Radigan . . . . Receptionist

Game By Game: The Giants

Giants 28, Cowboys 31
at Texas Stadium — September 8

Giants............. 0 14 7 7 — 28
Cowboys........... 0 17 0 14 — 31

COWBOYS — Dorsett 36 pass from D. White (Septien kick); COWBOYS — Walker 1 run (Septien kick); GIANTS — B. Johnson 13 pass from Simms (Thomas kick); GIANTS — Robinson 3 pass from Simms (Thomas kick); GIANTS — Morris 2 run (Thomas kick); COWBOYS — Chandler 1 pass from D. White (Septien kick); GIANTS — B. Johnson 44 pass from Simms (Thomas kick); COWBOYS — Walker 10 run (Septien kick).

TEAM STATISTICS
	Giants	Cowboys
First Downs	24	22
Total Net Yards	416	392
Net Yards Rushing	116	113
Net Yards Passing	268	285
Passes (Comp/Att/Int)	22-45-1	23-39-0
Punts Average	7-45.7	8-43.5
Fumbles Lost	2-1	2-2
Penalties-Yards	5-56	9-93

INDIVIDUAL STATISTICS
Rushing
GIANTS — Morris 20-87; Simms 2-10; Rouson 2-9; Carthon 3-8; Galbreath 1-2.
COWBOYS — Walker 10-64; Dorsett 8-25; Newsome 2-14; Lavette 2-6; D. White 1-4.
Passing
GIANTS — Simms 2-45, 300, 3TDs.
COWBOYS — D. White 23-39, 279, 2 TDS; Pelluer 0-1.
Receiving
GIANTS — B. Johnson 8-115; Bavaro 7-88; Robinson 3-48; Galbreath 2-11; Manuel 1-19; Miller 1-19.
COWBOYS — Walker 6-32; Hill 5-107; Newsome 5-22; Banks 2-41; Cosbie 2-24; Dorsett 1-26; Sherrard 1-16; Chandler 1-1.

Giants 20, Chargers 7
at Giants Stadium — September 14

Chargers.......... 0 7 0 0 — 7
Giants............. 3 7 0 10 — 20

GIANTS — FG Cooper 21; GIANTS — Morris 1 run (Cooper kick); CHARGERS — Anderson 29 pass from Fouts (Benirschke kick); GIANTS — Manuel 12 pass from Simms (Cooper kick); GIANTS — FG Cooper 20.

TEAM STATISTICS
	Chargers	Giants
First Downs	18	25
Total Net Yards	265	391
Net Yards Rushing	41	134
Net Yards Passing	221	257
Passes (Comp/Att/Int)	19-43-5	18-38-1
Punts Average	4-47.5	5-39.8
Fumbles Lost	3-2	4-0
Penalties-Yards	5-27	6-61

INDIVIDUAL STATISTICS
Rushing
CHARGERS — McGee 5-19; Anderson 3-10; Spencer 2-6; James 3-6.
GIANTS — Morris 30-83; Manuel 1-25; Carthon 8-23; Rouson 3-10; Simms 3-(-7).
Passing
CHARGERS — Fouts 19-43, 224, 1 TD.
GIANTS — Simms 18-37, 300, 1 TD; Galbreath 0-1.
Receiving
CHARGERS — Chandler 4-58; Anderson 4-45; Winslow 4-39; McGee 4-37; Joiner 1-20; Johnson 1-20; Holohan 1-10.
GIANTS — Bavaro 5-89; Robinson 4-69; Manuel 3-71; Morris 3-35; Miller 1-21; Galbreath 1-11; Carthon 1-4.

Giants 14, Raiders 9
at Los Angeles Coliseum — September 21

Giants............. 0 0 7 7 — 14
Raiders........... 6 0 0 3 — 9

RAIDERS — FG Bahr 22; RAIDERS — FG Bahr 35; GIANTS — Manuel 18 pass from Simms (Cooper kick); GIANTS — Manuel 11 pass from Simms (Cooper kick); RAIDERS — FG Bahr 33.

TEAM STATISTICS
	Giants	Raiders
First Downs	18	14
Total Net Yards	334	318
Net Yards Rushing	129	58
Net Yards Passing	205	260
Passes (Comp/Att/Int)	18-30-2	21-41-0
Punts Average	5.49.0	5-38.8
Fumbles Lost	0-0	2-2
Penalties-Yards	6-35	9-50

INDIVIDUAL STATISTICS
Rushing
GIANTS — Morris 18-110; Carthon 3-12; Rouson 1-4; Galbreath 1-4; Hostetler 1-1; Simms 1-(-2).
RAIDERS — Allen 15-40; Mueller 2-5; D. Williams 1-5; Hawkins 1-4; Plunkett 2-4; Strachan 1-0.
Passing
GIANTS — Simms 18-30, 239, 2 TDs.
RAIDERS — Plunkett 21-41, 281.
Receiving
GIANTS — Bavaro 6-106; Manuel 6-81; Galbreath 4-13; Robinson 2-39.
RAIDERS — Allen 5-86; Mueller 4-28; Christensen 4-27; Hawkins 3-16; Hester 2-44; Junkin 2-38; D. Williams 1-42.

Giants 20, Saints 17
at Giants Stadium — September 28

Saints............ 14 3 0 0 — 17
Giants............ 0 10 3 7 — 20

SAINTS — Martin 63 pass from Wilson (Andersen kick); SAINTS — Hilliard 1 run (Andersen kick); SAINTS — FG Andersen 27; GIANTS — FG Allegre 29; GIANTS — Bavaro 19 pass from Simms (Allegre kick); GIANTS — FG Allegre 28; GIANTS — Mowatt 4 pass from Simms (Allegre kick).

TEAM STATISTICS
	Saints	Giants
First Downs	10	26
Total Net Yards	196	388
Net Yards Rushing	65	114
Net Yards Passing	131	274
Passes (Comp/Att/Int)	12-20-0	24-41-3
Punts Average	7-44.0	3-44.7
Fumbles Lost	4-1	4-0
Penalties-Yards	8-54	11-94

INDIVIDUAL STATISTICS
Rushing
SAINTS — Mayes 10-31; Hilliard 11-27; Jordan 3-7; Wilson 1-0.
GIANTS — Rouson 24-71; Simms 4-28; Carthon 4-12; Miller 1-3.
Passing
SAINTS — Wilson 12-20, 146, 1 TD.
GIANTS — Simms 24-41, 286, 2 TDs.
Receiving
SAINTS — Brenner 3-30; Martin 2-67; Jones 2-23; Mayes 2-12; Jordan 2-10; Hilliard 1-4.
GIANTS — Bavaro 7-110; Robinson 4-66; Mowatt 4-48; Rouson 3-13; Johnson 2-16; Carthon 2-7; Miller 1-7; Galbreath 1-7.

Giants 13, Cardinals 6
at Busch Stadium — October 5

Giants............. 0 6 7 0 — 13
Cardinals......... 3 0 3 0 — 6

CARDINALS — FG Lee 31; GIANTS — FG Allegre 44; GIANTS — FG Allegre 31; GIANTS — Morris 1 run (Allegre kick); CARDINALS — FG Lee 47.

TEAM STATISTICS
	Giants	Cardinals
First Downs	8	12
Total Net Yards	144	241
Net Yards Rushing	61	83
Net Yards Passing	83	158
Passes (Comp/Att/Int)	8-24-0	17-30-1
Punts Average	9-47.0	8-38.0
Fumbles Lost	3-1	4-1
Penalties-Yards	8-55	10-100

INDIVIDUAL STATISTICS
Rushing
GIANTS — Morris 17-53; Carthon 2-9; Galbreath 2-7; Simms 4-(-8).
CARDINALS — Anderson 18-55; Ferrell 12-29; Lomax 1-0; Mitchell 1-(-1).
Passing
GIANTS — Simms 8-24, 104.
CARDINALS — Lomax 17-30, 206.
Receiving
GIANTS — Galbreath 3-30; B. Johnson 2-55; Bavaro 2-16; Carthon 1-3.
CARDINALS — J.T. Smith 4-95; Marsh 4-45; Mitchell 3-30; Ferrell 3-21; Anderson 3-15.

Giants 35, Eagles 3
at Giants Stadium — October 12

Eagles............ 0 3 0 0 — 3
Giants............ 0 14 14 7 — 35

GIANTS — Morris 30 run (Allegre kick); EAGLES — FG McFadden 29; GIANTS — Simms 4 run (Allegre kick); GIANTS — Miller 10 pass from Simms (Allegre kick); GIANTS — Carson 13 pass from Rutledge (Allegre kick); GIANTS — Rouson 37 pass from Simms (Allegre kick).

TEAM STATISTICS
	Eagles	Giants
First Downs	9	24
Total Net Yards	117	394
Net Yards Rushing	59	178
Net Yards Passing	58	216
Passes (Comp/Att/Int)	9-28-1	21-30-0
Punts Average	8-37.6	5-39.8
Fumbles Lost	1-1	1-1
Penalties-Yards	7-60	13-70

INDIVIDUAL STATISTICS
Rushing
EAGLES — Byars 11-27; Cunningham 2-24; Haddix 4-8.
GIANTS — Morris 19-69; Carthon 7-43; Anderson 7-32; Rouson 9-26; Galbreath 1-7; Simms 2-4; Rutledge 1-(-3).
Passing
EAGLES — Jaworski 6-22, 50; Cunningham 3-6, 48.
GIANTS — Simms 20-29, 214, 2 TDs; Rutledge 1-1, 13, 1 TD.
Receiving
EAGLES — Spagnola 4-40; Johnson 1-38; Quick 1-9; Jackson 1-7; Toney 1-3; Tautalatasi 1-1.
GIANTS — Mowatt 3-41; Robinson 3-41; Bavaro 3-22; Galbreath 3-17; McConkey 2-26; Miller 2-22; Rouson 1-37; Carson 1-13; Morris 1-6; Carthon 1-3; Anderson 1-(-1).

Giants 12, Seahawks 17
at Seattle Kingdome — October 19

Giants............. 0 9 0 3 — 12
Seahawks.......... 7 0 3 7 — 17

SEAHAWKS — Hudson 16 pass from Krieg (N. Johnson kick); GIANTS — Miller 32 pass from Simms (kick failed); GIANTS — FG Allegre 23; SEAHAWKS — FG N. Johnson 25; SEAHAWKS — Warner 1 run (N. Johnson kick); GIANTS — FG Allegre 31.

TEAM STATISTICS
	Giants	Seahawks
First Downs	22	13
Total Net Yards	307	218
Net Yards Rushing	162	72
Net Yards Passing	145	146
Passes (Comp/Att/Int)	14-25-4	15-22-1
Punts Average	3-44.3	5-38.8
Fumbles Lost	1-0	2-1
Penalties-Yards	3-15	6-50

INDIVIDUAL STATISTICS
Rushing
GIANTS — Morris 24-116; Carthon 10-35; Galbreath 3-7; Rouson 1-4.
SEAHAWKS — Warner 19-56; Williams 5-17; Krieg 3-(-1).
Passing
GIANTS — Simms 14-25, 190, 1 TD
SEAHAWKS — Krieg 15-22, 166, 1 TD.
Receiving
GIANTS — B. Johnson 3-49; McConkey 3-49; Miller 3-46; Morris 1-23; Rouson 1-11; Galbreath 1-8; Mowatt 1-6; Carthon 1-(-2).
SEAHAWKS — Warner 4-31; Franklin 2-46; Largent 2-20; Williams 2-19; Turner 2-16; Hudson 1-16; Tice 1-10; R. Butler 1-8.

Giants 27, Redskins 20
at Giants Stadium — October 27

Redskins.......... 0 3 14 3 — 20
Giants............. 3 10 7 7 — 27

GIANTS — FG Allegre 37; GIANTS — Morris 11 run (Allegre kick); REDSKINS — FG Zendejas 23; GIANTS — FG Allegre 44; GIANTS — Johnson 30 pass from Simms (Allegre kick); REDSKINS — Rogers 1 run (Zendejas kick); REDSKINS — Clark 42 pass from Schroeder (Zendejas kick); REDSKINS — FG Zendejas 29; GIANTS — Morris 13 run (Allegre kick).

TEAM STATISTICS
	Redskins	Giants
First Downs	17	24
Total Net Yards	410	397
Net Yards Rushing	32	202
Net Yards Passing	378	195
Passes (Comp/Att/Int)	22-40-2	20-30-0
Punts Average	4-50.0	6-43.2
Fumbles Lost	1-0	0-0
Penalties-Yards	8-41	5-45

INDIVIDUAL STATISTICS
Rushing
REDSKINS — Rogers 16-30; Schroeder 1-2; Griffin 1-0.
GIANTS — Morris 31-181; Galbreath 1-10; Carthon 2-7; Anderson 2-6; Simms 1-(-2).
Passing
REDSKINS — Schroeder 22-40, 420, 1 TD.
GIANTS — Simms 20-30, 219, 1 TD.
Receiving
REDSKINS — Clark 11-241; Monk 3-59; Warren 3-18; Didier 2-17; Sanders 1-71; Rogers 1-13; Griffin 1-1.
GIANTS — Morris 5-59; Galbreath 5-54; Bavaro 5-41; Johnson 3-53; Anderson 2-12.

Giants 17, Cowboys 14
at Giants Stadium — November 2

Cowboys........... 0 7 0 7 — 14
Giants............. 3 7 0 7 — 17

GIANTS — FG Allegre 25; COWBOYS — Renfro 11 pass from Pelluer (Septien kick); GIANTS — Morris 8 run (Allegre kick); GIANTS — Morris 6 run (Allegre kick); COWBOYS — Dorsett 23 run (Septien kick).

TEAM STATISTICS
	Cowboys	Giants
First Downs	25	14
Total Net Yards	408	245
Net Yards Rushing	102	199
Net Yards Passing	306	46
Passes (Comp/Att/Int)	29-41-0	6-18-1
Punts Average	4-24.5	4-46.3
Fumbles Lost	4-3	2-2
Penalties-Yards	9-103	5-44

INDIVIDUAL STATISTICS
Rushing
COWBOYS — Dorsett 10-45; Walker 10-34; Pelluer 3-19; Newsome 1-4; White 1-0.
GIANTS — Morris 29-181; Anderson 4-12; Carthon 2-10; Simms 2-(-4).
Passing
COWBOYS — D. White 1-3, 8; Pelluer 28-38, 339, 1 TD.
GIANTS — Simms 6-18, 67.
Receiving
COWBOYS — Walker 9-148; Newsome 7-28; Hill 5-75; Renfro 4-45; Cosbie 2-29; Sherrard 1-21; Lavette 1-1.
GIANTS — Bavaro 3-47; McConkey 1-10; Johnson 1-8; Mowatt 1-2.

Giants 17, Eagles 14
at Veterans Stadium — November 9

Giants............. 0 10 7 0 — 17
Eagles............ 0 0 0 14 — 14

GIANTS — Morris 18 run (Allegre kick); GIANTS — FG Allegre 22; GIANTS — Morris 3 run (Allegre kick); EAGLES — Quick 75 pass from Cunningham (McFadden kick); EAGLES — Cunningham 1 run (McFadden kick).

	Giants	Eagles
First Downs	15	17
Total Net Yards	265	237
Net Yards Rushing	153	78
Net Yards Passing	112	159
Passes (Comp/Att/Int)	8-18-2	18-36-2
Punts Average	7-45.4	7-37.7
Fumbles Lost	1-0	0-0
Penalties-Yards	9-74	6-60

INDIVIDUAL STATISTICS
Rushing
GIANTS—Morris 27-111; Carthon 7-31; Simms 5-10; Galbreath 1-1.
EAGLES—Cunningham 4-42; Crawford 5-17; Haddix 5-12; Byars 1-8; Jaworski 1-3; Tautalatasi 2-(-4).
Passing
GIANTS—Simms 8-18, 130.
EAGLES—Jaworski 8-15, 50; Cunningham 10-21, 152, 1 TD.
Receiving
GIANTS—Bavaro 4-76; Morris 2-25; Miller 1-17; Galbreath 1-12.
EAGLES—Tautalatasi 11-86; Quick 3-86; Haddix 2-0; Garrity 1-18; Jackson 1-12.

Giants 22, Vikings 20
at Hubert H. Humphrey Metrodome — November 16

Giants	3	6	3	10	— 22
Vikings	3	3	7	7	— 20

GIANTS—FG Allegre 41; VIKINGS—FG C. Nelson 39; GIANTS—FG Allegre 37; VIKINGS—FG C. Nelson 44; VIKINGS—FG Allegre 24; VIKINGS—Rice 8 pass from Kramer (C. Nelson kick); GIANTS—FG Allegre 37; GIANTS—B. Johnson 25 pass from Simms (Allegre kick); VIKINGS—Carter 33 pass from Wilson (C. Nelson kick); GIANTS—FG Allegre 33.
TEAM STATISTICS

	Giants	Vikings
First Downs	23	21
Total Net Yards	383	353
Net Yards Rushing	90	109
Net Yards Passing	293	244
Passes (Comp/Att/Int)	25-38-2	20-31-0
Punts Average	2-55.5	4-47.5
Fumbles Lost	1-0	1-1
Penalties-Yards	5-25	8-108

INDIVIDUAL STATISTICS
Rushing
GIANTS—Morris 18-49; B. Johnson 1-22; Simms 3-18; Carthon 3-1.
VIKINGS—D. Nelson 13-68; A. Anderson 4-14; Rice 4-13; Kramer 3-9; Wilson 1-5.
Passing
GIANTS—Simms 25-38, 310, 1 TD.
VIKINGS—Kramer 16-25, 187, 1 TD; Wilson 4-6, 68, 1 TD.
Receiving
GIANTS—Bavaro 4-81; B. Johnson 4-79; O. Anderson 4-19; Morris 3-27; Galbreath 3-26; Carthon 3-14; McConkey 2-41; Robinson 2-23.
VIKINGS—Jordan 5-77; Carter 4-71; D. Nelson 4-23; Lewis 3-46; Rice 3-29; Anderson 1-9.

Giants 19, Broncos 16
at Giants Stadium — November 23

Broncos	3	3	7	3	— 16
Giants	0	10	3	6	— 19

BRONCOS—FG Karlis 40; GIANTS—FG Allegre 31; BRONCOS—FG Karlis 32; GIANTS—Martin 78 interception return (Allegre kick); GIANTS—FG Allegre 45; BRONCOS—FG Karlis 42; GIANTS—FG Allegre 46; BRONCOS—Winder 4 run (Karlis kick); GIANTS—FG Allegre 34.
TEAM STATISTICS

	Broncos	Giants
First Downs	26	14
Total Net Yards	405	262
Net Yards Rushing	80	143
Net Yards Passing	325	119
Passes (Comp/Att/Int)	29-48-2	11-20-0
Punts Average	3-34.3	6-48.8

Fumbles Lost 2-2   2-2
Penalties-Yards 4-60   9-89
INDIVIDUAL STATISTICS
Rushing
BRONCOS—Elway 8-51; Winder 13-24; Willhite 1-5.
GIANTS—Morris 23-106; Simms 5-20; Rouson 2-9; Galbreath 3-7; Carthon 3-1.
Passing
BRONCOS—Elway 29-47, 336.
GIANTS—Simms 11-20, 148.
Receiving
BRONCOS—Winder 6-31; Willhite 5-42; Mobley 4-49; M. Jackson 3-47; Johnson 3-47; Kay 3-34; Watson 2-38; Lang 2-17; Sampson 1-31.
GIANTS—McConkey 2-54; Morris 2-16; Carthon 2-13; Johnson 1-24; Bavaro 1-15; Robinson 1-15; Galbreath 1-7; Anderson 1-4.

Giants 21, 49ers 17
at Candlestick Park — December 1

Giants	0	0	21	0	— 21
49ers	3	14	0	0	— 17

49ERS—FG Wersching 30; 49ERS—Rice 11 pass from Montana (Wersching kick); Rice 1 run (Wersching kick); GIANTS—Morris 17 pass from Simms (Allegre kick); GIANTS—Robinson 34 pass from Simms (Allegre kick); GIANTS—Anderson 1 run (Allegre kick).
TEAM STATISTICS

	Giants	49ers
First Downs	20	26
Total Net Yards	397	367
Net Yards Rushing	13	116
Net Yards Passing	384	251
Passes (Comp/Att/Int)	27-38-2	32-52-1
Punts Average	3-41.0	5-42.8
Fumbles Lost	2-1	1-0
Penalties-Yards	1-5	6-25

INDIVIDUAL STATISTICS
Rushing
GIANTS—Morris 13-14; Carthon 1-1; Anderson 2-1; Simms 3-(-1).
49ERS—Tyler 13-59; Craig 10-43; Cribbs 2-11; Montana 1-2; Rice 1-1.
Passing
GIANTS—Simms 27-38, 388, 2 TDs.
49ERS—Montana 32-52, 251, 1 TD.
Receiving
GIANTS—Bavaro 7-98; Robinson 5-116; Morris 4-42; Galbreath 3-55; Carthon 3-13; McConkey 2-46; B. Johnson 2-26; Morris 1-12.
49ERS—Craig 12-75; Rice 9-86; Francis 5-39; Clark 3-33; Cribbs 1-8; Crawford 1-5; Frank 1-5.

Giants 24, Redskins 14
at RFK Stadium — December 7

Giants	0	14	10	0	— 24
Redskins	0	7	0	7	— 14

GIANTS—Bavaro 9 pass from Simms (Allegre kick); REDSKINS—Bryant 4 run (Zendejas kick); GIANTS—B. Johnson 7 pass from Simms (Allegre kick); GIANTS—FG Allegre 21; GIANTS—McConkey 16 pass from Simms (Allegre kick); REDSKINS—Bryant 22 pass from Schroeder (Zendejas kick).
TEAM STATISTICS

	Giants	Redskins
First Downs	17	22
Total Net Yards	333	349
Net Yards Rushing	74	73
Net Yards Passing	259	276
Passes (Comp/Att/Int)	15-29-2	28-51-6
Punts Average	6-37.3	3-35.3
Fumbles Lost	1-0	3-1
Penalties-Yards	2-15	2-9

INDIVIDUAL STATISTICS
Rushing
GIANTS—Morris 22-62; Galbreath 2-9; Carthon 2-4; Rouson 2-1; Simms 4-(-2).
REDSKINS—Bryant 6-50; Rogers 10-22; Schroeder 1-1.
Passing
GIANTS—Simms 15-29, 265, 3 TDs.

REDSKINS—Schroeder 28-51, 309, 1 TD.
Receiving
GIANTS—Bavaro 5-111; B. Johnson 3-60; McConkey 2-24; Galbreath 2-22; Rouson 1-21; Robinson 1-19; Carthon 1-8.
REDSKINS—Bryant 13-130; Monk 5-40; Warren 4-27; Clark 3-73; Griffin 2-30; Sanders 1-9.

Giants 27, Cardinals 7
at Giants Stadium — December 14

Cardinals	0	0	0	7	— 7
Giants	7	10	3	7	— 27

GIANTS—Morris 2 run (Allegre kick); GIANTS—Morris 3 run (Allegre kick); GIANTS—FG Allegre 26; GIANTS—FG Allegre 23; CARDINALS—R. Green 15 pass from Mitchell (Schubert kick); GIANTS—Morris 1 run (Allegre kick).
TEAM STATISTICS

	Cardinals	Giants
First Downs	15	20
Total Net Yards	184	313
Net Yards Rushing	84	251
Net Yards Passing	100	62
Passes (Comp/Att/Int)	21-28-1	5-21-0
Punts Average	8-34.4	6-41.8
Fumbles Lost	3-1	4-2
Penalties-Yards	9-44	2-10

INDIVIDUAL STATISTICS
Rushing
CARDINALS—Mitchell 11-46; Ferrell 6-23; Lomax 3-15.
GIANTS—Morris 28-179; Carthon 8-34; Simms 4-10; Anderson 3-9; Rouson 2-6; Galbreath 1-7; B. Johnson 1-6.
Passing
CARDINALS—Lomax 20-27, 153; Mitchell 1-1, 15, 1 TD.
GIANTS—Simms 5-21, 82.
Receiving
CARDINALS—R. Green 5-40; Ferrell 5-34; Mitchell 5-25; J.T. Smith 4-42; Marsh 2-27.
GIANTS—Bavaro 2-42; Robinson 1-19; Johnson 1-15; McConkey 1-6.

Giants 55, Packers 24
at Giants Stadium — December 20

Packers	0	17	7	0	— 24
Giants	21	3	14	17	— 55

GIANTS—Bavaro 24 pass from Simms (Allegre kick); GIANTS—Flynn 36 run with blocked punt (Allegre kick); GIANTS—Morris 3 run (Allegre kick); GIANTS—FG Allegre 46; PACKERS—Ivery 13 pass from Wright (Del Greco kick); PACKERS—Stills 58 interception return (Del Greco kick); PACKERS—FG Del Greco 34; GIANTS—Bavaro 4 pass from Simms (Allegre kick); PACKERS—Davis 15 pass from Wright (Del Greco kick); GIANTS—Mowatt 22 pass from Simms (Allegre kick); GIANTS—Rouson 10 run (Allegre kick); GIANTS—Rouson 21 run (Allegre kick); GIANTS—FG Allegre 26.
TEAM STATISTICS

	Packers	Giants
First Downs	17	30
Total Net Yards	314	448
Net Yards Rushing	119	226
Net Yards Passing	195	222
Passes (Comp/Att/Int)	19-36-2	18-27-2
Punts Average	6-35.0	2-55.0
Fumbles Lost	2-1	2-0
Penalties-Yards	14-94	5-40

INDIVIDUAL STATISTICS
Rushing
PACKERS—Davis 8-92; Carruth 9-21; Ellis 2-6.
GIANTS—Morris 22-115; Rouson 8-39; Carthon 7-29; Rutledge 2-22; Anderson 6-21.
Passing
PACKERS—Wright 19-36, 199, 2 TDs.
GIANTS—Simms 18-25, 245, 3 TDs; Rutledge 0-2.
Receiving
PACKERS—Davis 6-45; Ivery 5-67; Ross 2-18; Carruth 2-17; Moffitt 1-34; Franz 1-7; Stanley 1-6; West 1-5.
GIANTS—Bavaro 5-59; Robinson 3-39; Galbreath

3-15; B. Johnson 2-44; Rouson 2-39; McConkey 1-23; Mowatt 1-22; Carthon 1-4.

NFC DIVISIONAL PLAYOFF
Giants 49, 49ers 3
at Giants Stadium — January 4, 1987

49ers	3	0	0	0	— 3
Giants	7	21	21	0	— 49

GIANTS—Bavaro 24 pass from Simms (Allegre kick); 49ERS—FG Wersching 26; GIANTS—Morris 45 run (Allegre kick); GIANTS—Johnson 15 pass from Simms (Allegre kick); GIANTS—Taylor 34 interception return (Allegre kick); GIANTS—McConkey 28 pass from Simms (Allegre kick); GIANTS—Mowatt 29 pass from Simms (Allegre kick); GIANTS—Morris 2 run (Allegre kick).
TEAM STATISTICS

	49ers	Giants
First Downs	9	21
Total Net Yards	184	366
Net Yards Rushing	29	216
Net Yards Passing	155	150
Passes (Comp/Att/Int)	15-37-3	10-20-0
Punts Average	10-40.0	7-43.9
Fumbles Lost	2-1	0-0
Penalties-Yards	11-62	3-23

INDIVIDUAL STATISTICS
Rushing
49ERS—Craig 5-17; Rathman 3-8; Cribbs 12-4.
GIANTS—Morris 24-159; Rouson 8-28; Carthon 6-17; Simms 1-15; Anderson 4-2; Manuel 1-(-5).
Passing
49ERS—Montana 8-15, 98; Kemp 7-22, 64.
GIANTS—Simms 9-19, 136, 4 TDs; Rutledge 1-1, 23.
Receiving
49ERS—Craig 4-22; Clark 3-52; Rice 3-48; Francis 3-26; Margerum 1-12; Cribbs 1-2.
GIANTS—Bavaro 2-47; Rouson 2-22; Mowatt 1-29; McConkey 1-28; B. Johnson 1-15; Galbreath 1-9; Carthon 1-7; Morris 1-2.

NFC CHAMPIONSHIP GAME
Giants 17, Redskins 0
at Giants Stadium — January 11, 1987

Redskins	0	0	0	0	— 0
Giants	10	0	7	0	— 17

GIANTS—FG Allegre 47; GIANTS—Manuel 11 pass from Simms (Allegre kick); GIANTS—Morris 1 run (Allegre kick).
TEAM STATISTICS

	Redskins	Giants
First Downs	12	12
Total Net Yards	190	199
Net Yards Rushing	40	117
Net Yards Passing	150	82
Passes (Comp/Att/Int)	20-50-1	7-14-0
Punts Average	9-35.6	6-42.3
Fumbles Lost	3-1	4-3
Penalties-Yards	3-15	6-48

INDIVIDUAL STATISTICS
Rushing
REDSKINS—Bryant 6-25; Rogers 9-15; Schroeder 1-0.
GIANTS—Morris 29-87; Carthon 7-28; Anderson 1-3; Rouson 1-2; Galbreath 1-(-1); Simms 7-(-2).
Passing
REDSKINS—Schroeder 20-50, 195.
GIANTS—Simms 7-14, 90, 1 TD.
Receiving
REDSKINS—Monk 8-126; Bryant 7-45; Warren 3-9; Griffin 1-8; Didier 1-7.
GIANTS—Carthon 3-18; Bavaro 2-36; Manuel 2-36.

Super Bowl XXI Play-By-Play

First Quarter
Denver wins the coin toss and elects to receive
New York will kick off and defend the north goal
Allegre kicks off to the DB1
Returned by Lang 23 yards to the DB24 (Flynn, Hunt)
Broncos Ball (15:00)
1-10, DB24: Elway back to pass, runs for 10 to DB34 (Carson)
1-10, DB34: Winder left side for 1 to DB35 (Marshall)
2-9, DB35: Willhite wide right for 2 to DB37 (Banks)
3-7, DB37: Elway passes to M. Jackson for 24 to NY39 (Collins)
1-10, NY39: Elway passes to Winder for 5 to NY34 (Reasons)
2-5, NY34: Winder right side for 3 to NY31 (Banks)
3-2, NY31: Winder right side for no gain (Banks)
Giants time out (1) 12 men on field
4-2, NY31: Karlis kicks a 48-yard field goal
Broncos scoring drive was 45 yds. in 8 plays and took 4:09

DENVER 3, NEW YORK 0
Karlis kicks off to the NY4
Returned by Rouson 18 yards to the NY22 (Dennison, Bell)
Giants Ball (10:51)
1-10, NY22: Simms passes to Manuel for 17 to NY39 (Wright)
1-10, NY39: Simms passes to Bavaro for 9 to NY48 (Wright)
2-1, NY48: Morris wide right for 11 to DB41 (Foley)
1-10, DB41: Simms passes to Morris for 2 to DB39 (Ryan, Wright)
2-8, DB39: *Giants Penalized* 10 yards for holding (Bavaro)
2-18, DB49: Morris right side for 8 to DB41 (Foley)
3-10, DB41: Simms passes to Robinson for 18 to DB23 (Wilson)
1-10, DB23: Morris right side for no gain (Mecklenburg, Hunley)
2-10, DB23: Simms passes to Bavaro for 17 to DB6 (Robbins)
1-6, DB6: Simms passes to Mowatt for 6 for a touchdown
Giants scoring drive was 78 yds. in 9 plays and took 5:24
Allegre kick

NEW YORK 7, DENVER 3
Allegre kicks off to the DB14
Returned by Bell 28 yards to the DB42 (Flynn)
Broncos Ball (5:27)
1-10, DB42: Elway passes to Winder for 14 to NY44 (Carson)
1-10, NY44: Elway passes to Mobley for 11 to NY33 (Carson, Patterson)
1-10, NY33: Elway passes to Winder for 9 to NY24 (Carson)
Giants Penalized 12 yards for late hit (Carson)
1-10, NY12: *Giants Penalized* 6 yards for unsportsmanlike conduct after hit (Taylor)
Denver time out (1)
1-6, NY6: Sewell wide right for -3 to NY9 (Patterson, Taylor)
2-9, NY9: Elway passes to V. Johnson for 5 to NY4 (Reasons)
3-4, NY4: Elway draw for 4 for a touchdown
Broncos scoring drive was 58 yds. in 6 plays and took 3:21
Karlis kick

DENVER 10, NEW YORK 7
Karlis kicks off to the NY7
Returned by Rouson 16 yards to the NY23 (Robbins)
Giants Ball (2:06)
1-10, NY23: Simms passes to Morris for 7 to NY30 (Townsend)
2-3, NY30: Morris left side for 4 to NY34 (Woodard, Lilly)

1-10, NY34: Anderson left side for -1 to NY33 (Ryan)
End Qtr.: Broncos 10, Giants 7

Second Quarter
Giants Ball (15:00)
2-11, NY33: Morris wide left for 8 to NY41 (Lilly)
3-3, NY41: Simms passes incomplete to McConkey
4-3, NY41: Landeta punts 59 yards into the end zone—no return
Broncos Ball (14:00)
1-10, DB20: Lang wide right for -2 to DB18 (Taylor)
2-12, DB18: Elway passes incomplete to Mobley
3-12, DB18: Elway passes to V. Johnson for 54 to NY28 (Welch)
1-10, NY28: Elway passes to Winder for 6 to NY22 (Williams)
2-4, NY22: Elway passes incomplete to Willhite
3-4, NY22: Elway passes to Mobley for 6 to NY16 (Welch)
1-10, NY16: Lang up the middle for 4 to NY12 (P. Johnson)
2-6, NY12: Elway passes to Lang for 4 to NY8 (Patterson)
3-2, NY8: Elway passes to Sewell for 7 to NY1 (Hill)
1-1, NY1: Elway wide right for -1 to NY2 (Taylor)
2-2, NY2: Willhite up the middle for no gain (Carson)
3-2, NY2: Winder wide left for -4 to NY6 (Banks)
4-6, NY6: Karlis's 23-yd. field-goal attempt is wide right
Giants Ball (7:40)
1-10, NY20: Simms passes to Bavaro for 12 to NY32 (Smith)
1-10, NY32: Simms passes to Robinson for 8 to NY40 (Hunley)
2-2, NY40: Carthon up the middle for 1 to NY41 (Jones)
3-1, NY41: Morris left side for 4 to NY45 (Haynes)
1-10, NY45: Simms passes to Carthon for 1 to NY46 (Woodard)
2-9, NY46: Morris draw for 1 to NY47 (Gilbert, Ryan)
3-8, NY47: Simms passes incomplete to Robinson
4-8, NY47: Landeta punts 38 yards to the DB15; Willhite fair catches at the DB15
Broncos Ball (3:33)
1-10, DB15: Elway sacked for a loss of 2 yards (Marshall)
2-12, DB13: Elway passes incomplete to Kay
Instant replay inconclusive—play stands
3-12, DB13: Elway sacked for a loss of 13 yards and a safety (Martin)

DENVER 10, NEW YORK 9
Horan kicks off to the NY28
Returned by Flynn—3 yards to the NY25 (Micho)
Giants Ball (2:36)
1-10, NY25: Simms passes to Morris for -1 to NY24 (Hunley)
Two minute warning
2-11, NY24: Simms passes to Carthon for 7 to NY31 (Ryan)
3-4, NY31: Simms passes incomplete to Bavaro
4-4, NY31: Landeta punts 41 yards to the DB28
Returned by Willhite 9 yards to the DB37 (Rouson)
Broncos Ball (1:05)
1-10, DB37: Elway passes incomplete to Sewell
2-10, DB37: Elway passes to Watson for 31 to NY32 (Patterson)
1-10, NY32: Elway passes to Willhite for 11 to NY21 (Taylor)
Denver time out (2) 0:43
1-10, NY21: Elway passes incomplete to Sewell
Instant replay—play stands
2-10, NY21: *Giants Penalized* 5 yards for offsides (Burt)

2-5, NY16: Elway passes incomplete to Willhite
3-5, NY16: Elway passes incomplete to Mobley
4-5, NY16: Karlis's 34-yd. field-goal attempt is wide right
Giants Ball (0:13)
1-10, NY16: Simms up the middle for -2 to NY18
End Qtr.: Broncos 10, Giants 9

Third Quarter
Giants have the second-half option and elect to receive
Broncos will kick off from the south goal
Karlis kicks off to the NY15
Returned by Rouson 22 yards to the NY37 (Harden)
Giants Ball (15:00)
1-10, NY37: Morris wide right for 3 to NY40 (Foley)
2-7, NY40: Simms passes to Carthon for 4 to NY44 (Townsend)
3-3, NY44: Morris wide left for 2 to NY46 (Wright)
4-1, NY46: Rutledge right side for 2 to NY48 (Ryan)
1-10, NY48: Simms passes to Morris for 12 to DB40 (Mecklenburg)
1-10, DB40: Simms passes to Rouson for 23 to DB17 (Foley, Mecklenburg)
1-10, DB17: Morris right side for 3 to DB14 (Woodard)
2-7, DB14: Simms passes to Carthon for 1 to DB13 (Wright)
3-6, DB13: Simms passes to Bavaro for 13 for a touchdown
Giants scoring drive was 63 yds. in 9 plays and took 4:52
Allegre kick

NEW YORK 16, DENVER 10
Broncos penalized 5 yards for offsides on the extra point
Giants penalized 5 yards for offsides on the kick-off (Patterson)
Allegre kicks off to the DB1
Returned by Lang 13 yards to the DB14 (Hunt)
Broncos Ball (10:08)
1-10, DB14: Elway passes incomplete to V. Johnson (Marshall)
2-10, DB14: Elway passes to V. Johnson for 5 to DB19 (Carson)
3-5, DB19: Elway passes incomplete to Willhite
4-5, DB19: Horan punts 42 yards to the NY39; returned by McConkey 25 yards to the DB36 (Woodard)
Giants Ball (9:01)
1-10, DB36: Morris wide right for 7 to DB29 (Ryan)
2-3, DB29: Morris wide right for -2 to DB31 (Woodard, Hunley)
3-5, DB31: Morris wide left for 9 to DB22 (Wilson)
1-10, DB22: Rouson up the middle for 1 to DB21 (Woodard)
2-9, DB21: Simms passes to Manuel for 9 to DB12 (Wright)
1-10, DB12: Carthon right side for 2 to DB10 (Mecklenburg)
2-8, DB10: Simms back to pass, runs for 5 to DB5 (Hunley, Woodard)
New York time out (1) (4:42)
3-3, DB5: Morris left side for 1 to DB4 (Ryan, Jones)
4-2, DB4: Allegre kicks a 21-yard field goal
Giants scoring drive was 32 yds. in 9 plays and took 5:07

NEW YORK 19, DENVER 10
Allegre kicks off into the end zone—no return
Broncos Ball (3:54)
1-10, DB20: Elway passes incomplete to Watson
2-10, DB20: Elway passes to Willhite for 8 to DB28 (Marshall, Patterson)
3-2, DB28: Elway passes incomplete to Mobley (Banks)

4-2, DB28: Horan punts 40 yards to the NY32; McConkey fair catches at the NY32
Giants Ball (2:38)
1-10-NY32: Morris right side for 2 to NY34 (Hunley)
2-8-NY34: Simms passes to Manuel for 17 to DB49 (Smith)
1-10, DB49: Morris wide right for 4 to DB45 (Hunley)
2-6, DB45: Simms passes to McConkey for 44 to DB1 (Haynes)
1-1, DB1: Morris wide right for 1 for a touchdown
Giants scoring drive was 68 yds. in 5 plays and took 2:14
Allegre kick

NEW YORK 26, DENVER 10
Allegre kicks off into the end zone—no return
Broncos Ball (0:24)
1-10, DB20: Elway sacked for a loss of 11 yards (Marshall); Elway's fumble recovered at the DB9 by Elway
End Qtr.: Broncos 10, Giants 26

Fourth Quarter
Broncos Ball (15:00)
2-21, DB9: *Broncos penalized* 4 yards for illegal motion (Lanier)
2-25, DB5: Elway's pass intercepted by Patterson at the DB35; returned—7 yards to the DB42 (Watson)
Giants penalized 10 yards for illegal block
Giants Ball (14:46)
1-10-NY48: Morris left side for no gain (Jones)
2-10-NY48: Simms passes to Robinson for 36 to DB16 (Smith, Mecklenburg)
1-10, DB16: Morris right side for 1 to DB15 (Jones)
2-9, DB15: *Broncos penalized* 14 yards for pass interference (Wright)
1-10, DB1: Morris wide right for no gain (Wright)
2-10, DB1: Simms sacked for a loss of 5 yards (Gilbert, Woodard)
3-15, DB6: Simms passes to McConkey for 6 for a touchdown
Giants scoring drive was 52 yds. in 6 plays and took 3:50
Allegre kick

NEW YORK 33, DENVER 10
Giants TD pass was a deflection from Bavaro to McConkey
Broncos penalized 5 yards for offsides on extra point
Allegre kicks off to the DB16
Returned by Bell 10 yards to the DB16 (P. Johnson)
Bell's fumble recovered at the DB16 by Hackett
Broncos Ball (10:56)
1-10, DB16: Elway passes to V. Johnson for 10 to DB26
1-10, DB26: Elway passes to Willhite for 4 to DB30 (Banks)
2-6, DB30: Elway passes to M. Jackson for 16 to DB46 (Banks)
1-10, DB46: Elway passes to Willhite for 5 to NY49 (Lasker)
2-5-NY49: Elway passes to M. Jackson for 11 to NY38
1-10-NY38: Sewell wide left for 12 to NY26 (Welch)
1-10-NY26: Willhite left side for 6 to NY20 (Banks)
2-4-NY20: Elway passes incomplete to Kay
3-4-NY20: Elway draw for 6 to NY14 (Collins)
1-10-NY14: Sewell wide right for -6 to NY20 (Banks)
2-16-NY20: Elway back to pass, runs for 8 to NY12 (Carson)
3-8-NY12: Elway draw for 2 to NY10 (Banks)
4-6-NY10: Karlis kicks a 27-yard field goal
Broncos scoring drive was 74 yds. in 13 plays and took 4:55

NEW YORK 33, DENVER 13
Karlis kicks off to the NY46

Giants' 1986 Final Statistics (16 Games)

Returned by B. Johnson 0 yards to the DB46
Giants Ball (6:01)
1-10, DB46: Rouson wide right for 18 to DB28 (Wilson)
1-10, DB28: Rouson left side for 3 to DB25 (Jones)
2-7, DB25: Carthon left side for 1 to DB24 (Ryan)
3-6, DB24: Simms wide left for 22 to DB2 (Haynes, Kragen)
1-2, DB2 Anderson up the middle for 2 for a touchdown
Giants scoring drive was 46 yds. in 5 plays and took 2:43
Allegre kick

NEW YORK 39, DENVER 13
Allegre kicks off to the DB11
Returned by Bell 20 yards to the DB31 (Headen)
Broncos Ball (3:18)
1-10, DB31: Willhite draw for 11 to DB42 (Banks, Collins)
1-10, DB42: Elway passes to Willhite for 11 to NY47 (Taylor)
1-10-NY47: Elway passes incomplete to Willhite
2-10-NY47: Elway passes incomplete to Willhite
3-10-NY47: Elway passes to V. Johnson for 47 for a touchdown
Broncos scoring drive was 69 yds. in 5 plays and took 1:12
Karlis kick

NEW YORK 39, DENVER 20
Karlis kicks onsides to the 44
No return
Giants Ball (2:06)
1-10, DB44: Galbreath right side for 6 to DB38 (Jones, Townsend)
2-4, DB38: Galbreath up the middle for 6 to DB32 (Smith)
1-10, DB32: Rutledge up the middle for -1 to DB33 (Woodard)
2-11, DB33 Galbreath up the middle for 7 to DB26 (Woodard)
3-4, DB26 Galbreath wide right for -2 to DB28 (Fletcher, Ryan)
4-6, DB28: Rutledge wide left for -1 to DB29 (Jones, Woodard)
Broncos Ball (0:44)
1-10, DB29: Kubiak passes to Sampson for 9 to DB38 (Jones)
2-1, DB38: Kubiak passes to Sewell for 5 to DB43 (Patterson)
1-10, DB43: Kubiak passes to Watson for 23 to NY34
1-10-NY34: Kubiak passes to Sampson for 11 to NY23
1-10-NY23: Kubiak sacked for a loss of 6 yards (Dorsey)
End Qtr.: Broncos 20, Giants 39

TEAM STATISTICS	GIANTS	OPPONENTS
TOTAL FIRST DOWNS	324	284
Rushing	127	78
Passing	171	177
Penalty	26	29
3rd Down: Made/Att.	85/228	75/212
4th Down: Made/Att.	10/14	2/11
TOTAL NET YARDS	5378	4757
Avg. Per Game	336.1	297.3
Total Plays	1076	996
Avg. Per Play	5.0	4.8
NET YARDS RUSHING	2245	1284
Avg. Per Game	140.3	80.3
Total Rushes	558	350
NET YARDS PASSING	3133	3473
Avg. Per Game	195.8	217.1
Tackled/Yards Lost	46/367	59/414
Gross Yards	3500	3887
Att./Completions	472/260	587/334
Completion Pct.	55.1	56.9
Had Intercepted	22	24
PUNTS/AVERAGE	79/44.8	89/39.3
NET PUNTING AVG.	37.1	34.5
PENALTIES/YARDS	96/738	120/988
FUMBLES/BALL LOST	31/10	36/19
TOUCHDOWNS	42	26
Rushing	18	10
Passing	22	15
Returns	2	1

SCORE BY PERIODS	1	2	3	4	OT	Total
GIANTS	40	130	106	95	0	371
OPPONENTS	39	84	37	76	0	236

SCORING	TDR	TDP	TDRt	PAT	FG	S	TP
Allegre	0	0	0	33/33	24/32	0	105(a)
Morris	14	1	0	0/0	0/0	0	90(b)
B. Johnson	0	5	0	0/0	0/0	0	30
Bavaro	0	4	0	0/0	0/0	0	24
Anderson, StL-Giants	3	0	0	0/0	0/0	0	18
Anderson, Giants	1	0	0	0/0	0/0	0	6
Manuel	0	3	0	0/0	0/0	0	18
Rouson	2	1	0	0/0	0/0	0	18
Miller	0	2	0	0/0	0/0	0	12
Mowatt	0	2	0	0/0	0/0	0	12
Robinson	0	2	0	0/0	0/0	0	12
Cooper	0	0	0	4/4	2/4	0	10
Carson	0	1	0	0/0	0/0	0	6
Flynn	0	0	1	0/0	0/0	0	6
Martin	0	0	1	0/0	0/0	0	6
McConkey	0	1	0	0/0	0/0	0	6
Simms	1	0	0	0/0	0/0	0	6
Thomas	0	0	0	4/4	0/1	0	4
GIANTS	18	22	2	41/42	26/37	0	371
OPPONENTS	10	15	1	26/26	18/25	0	236

a-6th in NFC
b-8th in NFC

FIELD GOALS	1-19	20-29	30-39	40-49	50+
Allegre	0/0	10/11	8/8	6/11	0/2
Cooper	0/0	2/2	0/1	0/1	0/0
Thomas	0/0	0/0	0/1	0/0	0/0
GIANTS	0/0	12/13	8/10	6/12	0/2
OPPONENTS	0/0	6/6	8/11	4/7	0/1

PUNTING	No.	Yds.	Avg.	TB	In 20	Lg.	Bk.
Landeta	79	3539	44.8(c)	11	24	61	0
GIANTS	79	3539	44.8	11	24	61	0
OPPONENTS	89	3499	39.3	7	15	59	1

c-led NFC

RUSHING	No.	Yds.	Avg.	Long	TD
Morris	341	1516(f)	4.4	54	14
Carthon	72	260	3.6	12	0
Anderson, StL-Giants	75	237	3.2	16	3
Anderson, Giants	24	81	3.4	16	1
Rouson	54	179	3.3	21t	2
Simms	43	72	1.7	18	1
Galbreath	16	61	3.8	10	0
B. Johnson	2	28	14.0	22	0
Manuel	1	25	25.0	25	0
Rutledge	3	19	6.3	18	0
Miller	1	3	3.0	3	0
Hostetler	1	1	1.0	1	0
GIANTS	558	2245	4.0	54	18
OPPONENTS	350	1284	3.7	50	10

f-2nd in NFC

RECEIVING	No.	Yds.	Avg.	Long	TD
Bavaro	66(g)	1001	15.2	41	4
Galbreath	33	268	8.1	19	0
B. Johnson	31	534	17.2	44t	5
Robinson	29	494	17.0	49	2
Morris	21	233	11.1	23	1
Anderson, StL-Giants	19	137	7.2	19	0
Anderson, Giants	9	46	5.1	12	0
McConkey	16	279	17.4	46	1
Carthon	16	67	4.2	10	0
Manuel	11	181	16.5	35	3
Mowatt	10	119	11.9	30	2
Miller	9	144	16.0	32t	2
Rouson	8	121	15.1	37t	1
Carson	1	13	13.0	13t	1
GIANTS	260	3500	13.5	49	22
OPPONENTS	334	3887	11.6	75t	15

g-7th in NFC

PUNT RETURNS	Ret.	FC	Yds.	Avg.	Long	TD
McConkey	32	12	253	7.9(h)	22	0
Collins	3	1	11	3.7	6	0
Galbreath	3	1	1	0.3	1	0
Manuel	3	6	22	7.3	12	0
GIANTS	41	20	287	7.0	22	0
OPPONENTS	41	14	386	9.4	61	0

h-9th in NFC

KICKOFF RETURNS	No.	Yds.	Avg.	Long	TD
McConkey	24	471	19.6	27	0
Collins	11	204	18.5	26	0
Miller	7	111	15.9	23	0
Hill	5	61	12.2	30	0
Rouson	2	21	10.5	12	0
Lasker	1	0	0.0	0	0
GIANTS	50	868	17.4	30	0
OPPONENTS	70	1362	19.5	57	0

INTERCEPTIONS	No.	Yds.	Avg.	Long	TD
Kinard	4	52	13.0	25	0
Williams	4	31	7.8	15	0
Hill	3	25	8.3	23	0
Reasons	2	28	14.0	18	0
Patterson	2	26	13.0	26	0
Welch	2	22	11.0	16	0
Martin	1	78	78.0	78t	1
Carson	1	20	20.0	20	0
P. Johnson	1	13	13.0	13	0
Headen	1	1	1.0	1	0
Collins	1	0	0.0	0	0
Flynn, G.B.-Giants	1	0	0.0	0	0
Lasker	1	0	0.0	0	0
Marshall	1	0	0.0	0	0
GIANTS	24	296	12.3	78t	1
OPPONENTS	22	218	9.9	58t	1

PASSING	Att.	Comp.	Yards	Comp. %	Yards/Att.	TD	TD %	Int.	Int. %	Long	Sack/Lost	Rating
Simms	468	259	3487	55.3	7.45	21	4.5	22	4.7	49	45/359	74.6(i)
Rutledge	3	1	13	33.3	4.33	1	33.3	0	0.0	13t	0/0	87.5
Galbreath	1	0	0	0.0	0.00	0	0.0	0	0.0		1/8	39.6
GIANTS	472	260	3500	55.1	7.42	22	4.7	22	4.7	49	46/367	75.0
OPPONENTS	587	334	3887	56.9	6.62	15	2.6	24	4.1	75t	59/414	68.6

i-4th in NFC

1986 Statistics *(continued)*

Photo Credits

SACKS:
Taylor 20½[d], Marshall 12[e], Banks 6½, Sally 3½, Martin 3, Headen 2½, Carson 2, Howard 2, P. Johnson 2, Burt 1, Hill 1, Kinard 1, Lasker 1, Williams 1.

GIANTS	59
OPPONENTS	46

d-led NFL
e-tied 5th in NFC

1986 TEAM RECORDS

MOST VICTORIES REGULAR SEASON 14
MOST CONSECUTIVE VICTORIES . . . . 9 (tie)
MOST VICTORIES AT HOME, SEASON 8
MOST POINTS SCORED FIRST PERIOD, GAME 21
MOST FIELD GOALS ATTEMPTED, GAME . . . . 6 (tie)

1986 INDIVIDUAL RECORDS

MOST YARDS RUSHING, SEASON
Joe Morris 1,516
MOST RUSHING ATTEMPTS, SEASON
Joe Morris 341
MOST GAMES, 100 YARDS RUSHING, CAREER
Joe Morris 16
MOST GAMES, 100 YARDS RUSHING, SEASON
Joe Morris 8
HIGHEST RUSHING AVERAGE, CAREER
Joe Morris 4.35
MOST RUSHING TOUCHDOWNS, CAREER
Joe Morris 40
MOST RUSHING TOUCHDOWNS, GAME
Joe Morris . . . . 3 (tie)
MOST 300-YARD PASSING GAMES, CAREER
Phil Simms 15
MOST 300-YARD PASSING GAMES, SEASON
Phil Simms . . . . 4 (tie)
MOST RECEPTIONS, TIGHT END, SEASON
Mark Bavaro 66
MOST RECEIVING YARDS, TIGHT END, SEASON
Mark Bavaro 1,001
MOST QUARTERBACK SACKS, SEASON
Lawrence Taylor 20½
MOST FIELD GOALS ATTEMPTED, GAME
Raul Allegre . . . . 6 (tie)
HIGHEST PUNTING AVERAGE, CAREER
Sean Landeta 43.8
MOST OPPONENT FUMBLES RECOVERED, GAME
Harry Carson . . . . 2 (tie)
MOST DEFENSIVE TOUCHDOWNS, LINEMAN, CAREER
George Martin 6*
*NFL Record

As they went 17-2 and won Super Bowl XXI, the Giants wore this insignia on their jerseys during the 1986 season to honor cornerback Carl (Spider) Lockhart. A Giants player from 1965-1975, Lockhart died of cancer in 1985. On the back of their helmets, they also wore number 38, in memory of fullback John Tuggle, who played from 1983-85, and died of cancer in 1986.